D0591436

Trumping the
Rape Culture
&
Sexual Assault

By
Alexandra Allred

Copyright © 2017 Alexandra Allred

All rights reserved.

ISBN-13: 978-1-941398-18-0

DEDICATION

How brave the women of 2016 and 2017 have been. With the Women's March and #MeToo movements taking off, the #TimesUp! is right on time! Although Tarana Burke created #MeToo in 2007, it was actress Alyssa Milano who is credited with bringing it to the masses with Twitter. It is and has been a team effort.

For anyone in law enforcement or who teaches self-defense, the number of women responding with a #MeToo has been no surprise. Women have been the victims of assault (in one degree or another) since time began. In fact, the picture on the back cover is that of the statue, The Rape of Proserpina, created in 1622 in Rome, Italy, where it rests today. In Greek mythology, Persephone, the daughter of Zeus and Demeter, was picking flowers in a field when Hades, God of the Underworld, kidnapped her and dragged her to the underworld to be his wife. Never mind that Zeus could and should have retrieved his daughter, we are left with the tidy little story of why and how we have seasons. Hades agreed to let Persephone return to our world six months out of the year, which is why our trees and flowers once again bloom. We're just not supposed to think about her hell when she returns to hell – like a good girl.

Having the courage to speak up, particularly against abusers in power, has always been incredibly difficult.

For women like Andrea Constand and many of the other Bill Cosby accusers, speaking out against "America's Dad" brought them brutal treatment. Today, for the girls and women who have found courage to speak out against leaders, especially against leaders in this political culture of no-accountability, their bravery must be praised.

We thank you, dear sisters!
We are with you.
#TimesUp!

CONTENTS

Acknowledgments   I

1 It Wasn't Me!   1

2 It Was You!   7

3 Unwanted Advances or Assault in Public   14

4 Frailty: Thy Name is Woman   20

5 The Case of Brock Turner   25

6 You Defying the Odds   28

7 Reaction and Inaction   35

8 Rebel Yell   41

9 The Don't-Mess-With-Me-Walk   50

10 Locker Room Talk Isn't Just Talk   55

11 The Girl's Club   59

12 Let's Hear it For the Boys   64

13 Fight, Flight or …. Freeze?   68

14 Trumping Rape Culture and the Art   71

     Of War

15 Game On!   76

References   83

About the Author   86

ACKNOWLEDGMENTS

Sadly, I can only 'thank' certain political figures who repeatedly assaulted, degraded, demoralized and then denied any wrongdoing as the catalyst for this book.

1
THAT WASN'T ME

Before we can discuss any kind of self-defense or proactive measures, before we launch into any discussion about why or how an assault takes places, we have to look at who the assailant is.

He can be young or old.

He can be black or white, slight in build or monstrously huge.

He can be a she.

When I teach self-defense, I ask my students to imagine their "bad guy." Everyone has a different idea of what scary is. Many white women will conjure up a large and looming black guy. Many black women will envision a bearded, Aryan-Nation-looking dude in a flannel shirt, khakis and boots. It's not wrong; it's not right. It is what it is because of media images, previous experiences, and/or horror stories we've all heard. For that reason, children most often dream of monsters or ghoulish-looking men rather than the clean cut, boy-next-door young man who is more accurately the child molester.

What I tell my students is, "Take that image that you have in your mind and toss it out the window."

Who could have ever imagined all the charges against comedian Bill Cosby, "America's Dad," accused of enticing wanna-be models and actresses to his room only to serve them knock-out drugs to rape them? Who could have believed the horrendous stories about the affable-looking Hollywood director Harvey Weinstein? Who would have ever thought that the soon-to-be president of the United States would brag that by virtue of being famous he could do whatever he wanted to women, saying, "They let you do it. You can do anything… Grab 'em by the p****.'"

Long has the argument been made, in defense of these men, that men of power do not have to assault women because they can have or buy whomever they want. But we know better. We know that aggression against women has very little to do with sexual

1

attraction for the actual female. Aggression against women is about the attacker. It is about power.

Attackers, particularly the more seasoned ones, can be very persuasive. They can attack first, and then be so remorseful that their victims will forgive them, even feel sorry for them. Attackers can convince their victims that the attack was a misunderstanding; that the victim gave out confusing vibes; that the victim was actually asking for it (consciously or not) and, therefore, the attacker was merely a victim of her ploys.

What the attacker does most effectively, however, is deny accountability.

"It wasn't me."

Initially when the now-famous "Access Hollywood" tape surfaced in October 2016, Donald Trump accepted responsibility, though using familiar I'm-not-really-responsible taglines of boys-will-be-boys, when he said, "I've never said I'm a perfect person, nor pretended to be someone that I'm not. I've said some things that I regret and the words released today on this more-than-a-decade-old video are one of them. Anyone who knows me knows these words don't reflect who I am. I said it, I was wrong, and I apologize." A year later, however, when he saw there were no real repercussions for his actions, he began denying it is him on the tape, continues to deny it is him, and has insinuated that the tape is a fake.[1]

It Wasn't Me!

Even though the attacker has been caught – on tape – and apologizes, his beacon of righteousness has nothing to do with the crime or his victim, the immorality or depravity of his actions. Rather, how his supporters react has everything to do with the attacker's next response.

Because the assault against the woman had nothing to do with the woman but everything to do with the attacker, there is no real need to consider the victim. Right? It's all about the response from the alleged attacker's supporters.

So whether the attacker is a CEO, a businessman, an athlete, a celebrity, a politician, or a guy down the street, all take their lead from their supporters. Far too often, even when there are multiple allegations, witnesses, and evidence of other people's knowledge and/or involvement in the crimes against women (and cover-ups), the men continue on with business as usual, denying everything and apologizing to no one. This was case with comedian Bill Cosby, NFL quarterback Ben Roethlisberger, politician Donald Trump and former judge and senate hopeful Roy Moore.

In the May 2010 *Sports Illustrated* story about Ben Roethlisberger entitled, *"Bad Behavior, Bad Judgement: What Entitlement Run Amok is Costing the Proud Steelers,"* spotlighted the lengths others will go to in an effort to cover-up alleged assaults. Despite a growing number of assault allegations lodged against Roethlisberger, and what some noted a growing sense of entitlement, the two rape accusations—one levied in civil court after an alleged attack at a Lake Tahoe hotel in 2008, later settled in 2012, the other allegedly committed in 2010 and dropped a month later after Georgia prosecutors declined to press charges, cleared Roesthlisberger to continue his professional career. At the time, Steelers legend and sports commentator Terry Bradshaw, said on national TV that Roethlisberger "disrespected women" and that the franchise should have "dumped" him. But in a 2017 update on Ben's changed behavior (he apologized publicly for the "disappointment and negative attention" caused by his infamously entitled antics), there still are and will always be fans who, as the SI article reported, will "be rooting for him even if he killed someone." [2]

For NBA superstar Kobe Bryant, despite blood, hair, semen DNA evidence, bruises on his victim's neck, just one week before Bryant's rape case was to go to trial, the accuser dropped all charges. If convicted, Bryant faced life in prison but after an affective assault on the victim's character and personal life by Bryant's legal team, in which his lawyer, Pamela Mackey "slipped" to reveal the victim's name and personal information, six times in open court. No surprise, the victim then received a flood of rape and death threats, and she very understandably wanted out. [3][4]

In terms of getting victims to come forward, sixty-six percent of women polled said they were more likely to report a rape if their identities would not be revealed. Because of the manner in which

3

rape/assault victims have been historically treated in the media, in court, and by the public, it is understandable that victims wish to remain anonymous. [5]

Even as Judge Roy Moore's people argue against fellow townsmen and women, police, store owners and clerks that "if" Roy did as the aforementioned claim, why had it taken the women so long to report it, many of Moore's accusers endure tremendous backlash for speaking out when they did.

Time and again, when a fanbase or support group tolerate bad behaviors, the alleged assailants have no need to show remorse. Why? They don't have to.

Predators assault women because they can, because people will look the other way (or maybe even help cover up their crimes). Bill is (or was) funny, Donald has money and Roy is a "Christian," so it was all okay. It was all okay because each man had a fanbase willing to sell out their principles, morality, even public safety for the betterment of their business, their sport, or their political affiliation.

This cannot be said enough times. Aggressive, unwanted behaviors are not about you. These behaviors are for and about the predator.

Who is the Aggressor/Predator and
What are the Signs to Look For?

There are no hard-and-fast rules when it comes to what a sexual predator looks like, but there are some general behaviors and attitudes that are typical with most. They are:

- Aggressors tend to be immature.
- Aggressors tend to be bullies, often in a passive/aggressive manner.
- Aggressors tend to be bad losers.
- Aggressors tend to become overly emotional about issues and are easily frustrated.
- Aggressors miss common social cues about personal space or proper etiquette.
- Aggressors rarely take responsibility for their own actions

and often blame others.

- In the event of "evidence," aggressors tend to claim the evidence or truths are false, made up, or conjured.
- Aggressors display a lack of empathy or understanding in regards to other people's feelings.
- Aggressors are self-centered.
- Aggressors are often entitled or possess a sense of entitlement.
- Aggressors crave power and always have to be in control. They may often yell over others to be heard and, even as adults, throw tantrums.
- Not surprisingly, aggressors often display sexually deviant behaviors and/or attitudes, such as blurting out a woman's physical attributes or how a woman should be handled in front of other people, including other women.
- And aggressors justify mean-spirited comments; they justify sexually explicit remarks about women; they justify demeaning comments about women: *She had that coming... but you would never be like that.*

As part of their 'It Wasn't Me!" disguise, aggressors are masters of deflection. There is a reason people always say, "I had no idea! He seemed like such a nice guy!" when learning a neighbor, friend or teacher is a sexual predator. Aggressors are often:

- Married, a family-man or "a really nice guy"
- Entrenched in their community as a trusted member
- Given to "jokes" about women and/or objectifying women but always appearing light-hearted and harmless
- Able to gain trust through familiarity
- Often a shoulder to lean on in times of crisis as this allows them to insinuate themselves in the community, the family, the workplace and, ultimately, into your personal life. They are often – belatedly – described as someone you could count on.

And now you're thinking, "Well, that's just great. Who can I trust?"

You need to learn to trust <u>you</u>! In the coming chapters, we will discuss why women do not listen to their own instincts and how to change that. But, before we do that, we must dispel the myths of why women *deserve* to be victims.

2
IT WAS YOU!

If she was really raped, why did it take her so long to tell anyone?

Women cry rape when they regret having sex or are embarrassed.

She's just looking for attention!

Women accuse celebrities and athletes of rape for a pay-out.

How is it rape if there wasn't sex?

How is it rape if she went to his room with him?

She knew what she was getting in to ... What woman goes to a hotel room to 'talk' to a man alone?

Did you see how she was dressed?

If she was really raped, she would have called the police.

In reality, only 2% of all rape and related sex charges are false (or falsified), whereas only about 40% of all rapes are ever reported to the authorities.[6] Why?

Victims Avoid Reporting

- Victims know their report will become public and they are already devastated and humiliated.
- Victims fear further shame/embarrassment from public scrutiny regarding their personal lives, from how they dress, where they work, who they were with, etc.
- Victims fear how family will react.
- Victims fear their aggressor (and fear retribution from a boss, neighbor, friend or family member).
- Victims are further confused/ashamed when the aggressor is someone they know and loved/liked.

The more powerful, popular and/or successful the attacker, the less likely there will be a conviction in favor of the victim. Bill Cosby's first sexual assault trial ended in a mistrial. Who knows if either he or Weinstein will ever be convicted?

Indeed, though, the reaction to the Weinstein allegations has been remarkable. Although the alleged assaults went on for decades, when several dozen fairly famous women came forward with accusations, it seems that the public – after so many high-profile cases -- had finally had enough. The action against Weinstein was swift and heavy. Weinstein was a pariah. All associates cut him off; he was denounced in Hollywood; he lost his business, income, and family as even more alleged victims came forward. There was no mercy, nor should there have been.

Still, unsurprisingly, as the #MeToo movement ignited, encouraging more victims to come forward with their stories, public commentary sites show that men are far less inclined to believe claims of rape, particularly if the accused is famous. Historically speaking, women have been viewed as deceitful or "hysterical" and cannot be trusted. It is so much easier to:

- Blame the woman or girl.
- Blame the accusers and those who assist the victim.
- Blame the media.

In an NBC News/*Wall Street Journal* poll conducted shortly after the release of the "Access Hollywood" tape of Trump bragging about assaulting women, nearly 70% of the respondents conceded Trump probably made unwanted advances against his alleged victims, but 64% said they would still vote for Trump. Again, historically speaking, the subject of sexual violence against women is seen as one of the burdens of being a woman. It is up to us – women – to not allow ourselves to be victims. The aggressor is able to absolve himself from any responsibility.

As ridiculous and unbelievable as it seems, the following continue to be reasons why rape is ignored and/or tolerated by so many. Read this list. Truly read this list. As you do, think about how often you have heard these remarks. Perhaps you have even said or thought them yourself.

Then ask yourself what this list says about how we value women. What does this list say about how women have been and continue to be treated by the public, by academic institutions, by businesses, and by individuals? In the last year, how many times have radio and television personalities roasted a woman for what she wore, ignoring that she was actually physically assaulted?

The following is a very thorough list of myths and misconceptions about rape prepared by the Department of Counseling & Professional Studies and Title IX Coordinator at the University of Southern Arkansas:

"She Asked For It"

1. If a woman is raped while she is drunk, she is at least somewhat responsible for letting things get out of control.

2. When women go around wearing lowcut tops or short skirts, they're just asking for trouble.

3. If a woman goes home with a man she doesn't know, it is her own fault if she is raped.

4. When a woman is a sexual tease, eventually she is going to get in trouble.

5. A woman who 'teases' men deserves anything that might happen.

6. When women are raped, it's often because the way they said 'no' was ambiguous.

7. A woman who dresses in skimpy clothes should not be surprised if a man tries to force her to have sex.

8. A woman who goes to the home or apartment of a man on the first date is implying that she wants to have sex.

9. A woman who goes to the home or apartment on their first date implies that she is willing to have sex.

10. When women go around braless or wearing short skirts and tight tops, they are just asking for trouble.

11. Women who get raped while hitchhiking get what they deserve.

12. A woman who is stuck-up and thinks she is too good to talk to guys on the street deserves to be taught a lesson.

13. If a woman gets drunk at party and has intercourse with a man she's just met there, she should be considered

'fair game' of other males at the party who want to have sex with her too, whether she wants to or not.

"It Wasn't Really Rape"

1. If a woman doesn't physically fight back, you can't really say it was rape.

2. A rape probably didn't happen if the woman has no bruises or marks.

3. If the rapist doesn't have a weapon, you really can't call it rape.

4. If a woman doesn't physically resist sex – even when protesting verbally – it really can't be considered rape.

5. If a woman claims to have been raped but has no bruises or scrapes, she probably shouldn't be taken too seriously.

6. Any healthy woman can resist a rapist if she really wants to.

"He Didn't Mean To"

1. When men rape, it is because of their strong desire for sex.

2. Rapists are usually sexually frustrated individuals.

3. When a man is very sexually aroused, he may not even realize that the woman is resisting.

4. Men don't usually intend to force sex on a woman, but sometimes they get too sexually carried away.

5. Rape happens when a man's sex drive gets out of control.

"She Wanted It"

1. Although most women wouldn't admit it, they generally find being physically forced into sex a real 'turn-on'.

2. Many women secretly desire to be raped.

3. Many women find being forced to have sex very arousing.

4. Some women prefer to have sex forced on them so they don't have to feel guilty about it.

5. Many women actually enjoy sex after the guy uses a little force.

6. If a girl engages in necking or petting and she lets things get out of hand, it is her own fault if her partner forces sex on her.

7. Many women have an unconscious wish to be raped, and may then unconsciously set up a situation in which they are likely to be attacked.

"She Lied"

1. Women who are caught having an illicit affair sometimes claim that it was rape.

2. Many so-called rape victims are actually women who had sex and 'changed their minds' afterwards.

3. Rape accusations are often used as a way of getting back at men.

4. A lot of women lead a man on and then they cry rape.

5. A lot of times, women who claim they were raped just have emotional problems.

6. One reason that women falsely report a rape is that they frequently have a need to call attention to themselves.

"Rape is a Trivial Event"

1. If a woman is willing to "make out" with a guy, then it's no big deal if he goes a little further and has sex.

2. Rape isn't as big a problem as some feminists would like people to think.

3. Being raped isn't as bad as being mugged and beaten.

4. Women tend to exaggerate how much rape affects them.

5. If a woman isn't a virgin, then it shouldn't be a big deal if her date forces her to have sex.

"Rape is a Deviant Event"

1. Rape mainly occurs on the 'bad' side of town.
2. Usually, it is only women who do things like hang out in bars and sleep around that are raped.
3. Men from nice middle-class homes almost never rape.
4. It is usually only women who dress suggestively that are raped.
5. Rape is unlikely to happen in the woman's own familiar neighborhood.
6. In reality, women are almost never raped by their boyfriends.
7. Rape almost never happens in the woman's own home.
8. Any female can get raped.
9. In the majority of rapes, the victim is promiscuous or has a bad reputation.

Infuriated? Disgusted?

During the 2016 Presidential elections in the U.S. while 'America's Dad' was under investigation for the dozens of allegations, and more and more women came forward with stories about Donald Trump, supporters of these men used to aforementioned arguments.

Remarkably, Trump himself joked that some of the women accusing him of sexual assault weren't pretty enough for him to have assaulted, that they weren't credible enough, that they just wanted attention, and so on.

What is clear is that the victim can never be enough. She wasn't valued when she was assaulted and she is often not valued when she reports the assault. *She had it coming. Why did she wait so long to report it? She just wants attention. She wants a pay-off. Where are the witnesses? Why didn't she say anything at the time? Where's the rape kit?*

In 2015, *USA Today* revealed that tens of thousands of rape kits sat collecting dust, untested, by different police agencies around the U.S.[7] In an investigative article entitled, "Why is rape so easy to get away with" (and published in *The Guardian*) journalist Julie Bindel looked at why rape victims "have only a tiny chance of seeing their attacker convicted."[8] Essentially, she found, the costs to departments, the courts, and the public aren't worth the trouble.

Further, it must be stated that even as the #MeToo movement has gathered momentum and garnered conversation and as we hope to bring greater awareness about this national and international crisis, statistics are not as optimistic for women of the working or lower economic classes, particularly among minorities. Blue collar women have higher instances of attack, are far less likely to report, and/or are far less likely to see results of a report.

Thus, the purpose of this book. While the hope is that every assault would be reported to bring about awareness, for better statistical evaluation and, most importantly, to bring sexual predators to justice, history proves otherwise. For these reasons, we cannot shame those who fear further indignation, shame, accusations, blame, even violence if they – the victims – speak out. This is not a platform to blame anyone except the excuses that allow for criminal and bad behaviors by attackers. This is an informational and motivational text to demonstrate how we, as women, can better protect ourselves. With awareness, we hope, can come change.

Your voice, your courage, your power and your tenacity can and will make a difference in your life and the lives of others. Power on.

3
UNWANTED ADVANCES
OR
AN ASSAULT IN PUBLIC

The following are real scenarios that must be presented so that we – together – can dissect what happened to one of our sisters, how it might have been handled differently, and how the aggressor sees himself in this scenario.

Scenario #1: Unwanted Advances or Assaults in Public

You're sitting on a fine velvet couch in a popular and very public nightspot when a person, perhaps someone you know or a stranger, sits down next to you and begins a conversation. At some point, he slides his hand up your skirt and touches you.

Let's stop right here.

Please note that just touching your knee or leg would be inappropriate and you would be very much in the right to say, "Please take your hand off of me. It makes me uncomfortable." This does not have to be said in anger, but your tone should be firm. No one has the right to tough you without your permission.

In this real-life scenario, however, the aggressor actually touches the woman's private parts.

Let's be clear: This is an assault.

In this particular situation, the woman was so stunned, she fell mute. This is (as we will later discuss) an extremely common reaction. In fact, there is actual science behind this reaction. Women are retractive. Women shrink away from such situations so that what they are experiencing is often later described as an out-of-body experience. *I couldn't believe it was happening* or *I didn't know what to do,* or *I kind of panicked.*

This woman later told friends what happened and, while all were perfectly horrified, no one called the authorities.

The aggressor knew his prey. He knew that this surprise ambush attack would render her stunned and helpless. He knew that by taking advantage of a public situation, she would either

14

respond in the manner he hoped or she would simply get away from him quietly and quickly. The latter is exactly what happened.

Predators choose their victims for a reason.

In this case, the aggressor was also supremely confident that his status and position in the community allowed him to behave as such.

What Should She Have Done?

Yelling, "What are you doing?" would have brought immediate attention to the situation.

This brings about a very dramatic shift in power.

Repeat: A dramatic shift in power.

You are in public. There is no way he can cause you any physical harm with so many witnesses. His 'thrill' was violating his prey in public and getting away with it. By yelling, bringing unwanted attention to him, stealing his "thrill" AND getting multiple witnesses to the assault, the power is now yours.

Next, police must be called. With witnesses still o]n hand, a formal complaint should be made. Witnesses are vital.

In this particular situation, the aggressor was wealthy and powerful. Such an aggressor banks on the victim being too embarrassed, too fearful of losing a job or losing status in the social scene to lodge any formal complaint.

What Would You Do?

Are you willing to lose your job with this person? Are you willing to lose your social status or even people you once considered friends in this scenario?

These are very real questions you need to ask yourself.

Scenario #2: Unwanted Advances or Assaults in Public

You are among a group of friends or colleagues when the aggressor makes his move. Women, no, people are often very slow to react in this scenario because of the group setting. It is hard to imagine that someone would do something egregious or inappropriate with so many people around. Therefore, there must be some kind of misunderstanding ... and with these feelings of confusion or uncertainty, no one reacts. The aggressor yields the power.

In this real-life situation, multiple teenagers in a Miss Teen USA competition were allegedly backstage dressing (and undressing) when an official with the competition walked in. When the underaged females scrambled to put on clothing, the aggressor responded that there was no need to worry as he had seen it all before.

This is a typical powerplay by an aggressor who pretends that his actions are innocent by deflecting all concerns: *I've seen it all before* or *please, I'm not even looking* or *I'm married, it's okay* or *don't flatter yourself.*

I'm-not-worried-about-it-so-you-shouldn't-worry-either game made the minors uncertain about the aggressors actions. They knew they did not like what just happened but was it morally wrong or illegal?

In this real-life scenario, the alleged complaint of Donald Trump walking backstage to find naked or half-dressed women scrambling to find clothing was repeated again and again during the Miss USA, Miss Universe and Teen competitions as, Trump himself bragged, he owned the pageants and had the right. This sense of entitlement became a game for him.[9] Though the young contestants called Trump, "Uncle Creepy,"[10] the predatory behavior continued and, it should be noted, among Miss Teen competitors.

What They Should Have Done

Full disclosure: There is no blame here. The girls did absolutely nothing wrong. They were victims of a predator who wanted to see underaged girls naked. They were so stunned, shocked and unclear about the rules of management and competition that they did the only thing they could think of: dress quickly. In an ideal world, however, had one of the victims taken a picture of the predator walking into the dressing area, it would have been far more difficult for him to explain to parents, the authorities (police and lawyers), and the public exactly why he walked into the dressing room of underage girls.

What Would You Do?

Do not get lost in this story. You do not have to have been in a beauty contest to experience this.

What if you were in the locker room with your fellow teammates and a male coach, assistant coach, school principal or teacher walked in while most of the team was naked? Further, what would you do if most of your teammates were unclothed, the male authority figure walked in and then, amidst the screams and scurrying, said, "Oh, whatever! I've seen it all before!"

Imagine that the coach laughed and made a joke of it, quickly turning to the 'business' of explaining where the bus was parked, when you had to be out on the field or court, etc. Does this make it okay to have walked in on a room of unclothed females?

Scenario #3: Unwanted Advances or Assault in Public

Was it assault?
What was that?

Quite often a woman is the victim of assault yet cannot wrap her mind around what just happened until much, much later. The incident can happen so quickly that the victim is left confused about what actually occurred. What she does know is that she did not like it and wants to get away from the aggressor.

In this real-life scenario, a woman is sitting in a public restaurant in a business setting. A group are seated at a round table when the aggressor finds ways to peer under the table to look up the skirts of other women seated at the table. He shares what he sees with the woman seated next to her, even asking her which of the women he should sleep with. He is in a position of great power and prior to the meeting, the woman wanted to impress this person.

What Should She Have Done?

Because he never touched her and, for that matter, because he never actually touched anyone in front of her, she was not sure what to do or how to respond. Instead, as was the aggressor's intention, she was mute. This passive listening (and again, no judgement against the woman who was, clearly, too stunned to react) is very exciting to the aggressor. Having a female audience listen to him discuss how to degrade and demoralize another female is classic predatory behavior.

What would have been both empowering to all the women at the table (especially for herself) and a de-masking of the monster seated with them would have been to ask loudly, "Are you seriously asking me which women you should sleep with?" All conversation would have stopped and the spotlight would have been placed on him – the monster. Even if he made a joke of it, claimed he had been misunderstood or appeared aghast that she could say such a thing, everyone at the table would forever remember that moment. These are not only potential witnesses to bad behavior for years to come but she would have alerted every woman (and man) at the table to the aggressor's true intentions.

What Would You Have Done?

In the previous scenario, a coach or teacher was inserted in the place of the businessman. The aggressor could also be a friend, an uncle, a neighbor, a pastor, or even (yes, this happens) a boyfriend. Understand this: This behavior does not and should never get a 'boys will be boys' pass. This is predatorial. This is demoralizing to all females involved. This is the behavior of a man who does not deem any female involved worthy of consideration beyond gratifying his own fantasy.

In the opening chapter, the reader is asked to describe what "your bad guy" looks like. Because, most likely, your neighbor, employer, business partner, coach, friend, or fellow student does not look like a 'bad guy,' you understand why so many girls and women feel both betrayed and confused by the aggressor in these scenarios.

He seemed like such a nice guy.
Why would he do that to me?
Why didn't I say something?

These are common responses to an all-too common occurrence of bad behaviors by bad men who just didn't look the part. So, it is time for you to take care of you.

We have defined "bad guy." A bad guy can be a stranger or someone you know.

A bad guy does not necessarily have a look, he has an agenda. The bad guy has a behavior. He dismisses and belittles women. He is opportunistic, using a public setting and your uncertainty to his advantage but you can trump your bad guy by adopting new behaviors of your own.

Define Self-Esteem.

What does self-esteem mean to you?

Define Strong.

What does the word strong mean to you?

Define Confident.

Are you confident? In what way?

Are you confident in how you move, how you walk or talk?

Having confidence in your appearance is certainly an empowering feeling but this will not save your life. You need to have confidence in your own voice. You need to have confidence in your abilities to speak up for yourself and defend your own honor.

Do you have these things in your self-defense armor?

Read on.

4
FRAILTY, THY NAME IS WOMAN

Though it is the Shakespearean line, 'Frailty, thy name is woman' from the play "Hamlet" that is most quoted, the word 'frailty' is used throughout the play and throughout history, almost exclusively connected to the state of a woman's physical, mental and moral being. It is always the woman who succumbs and ultimately lures the man into a state of weakness and, then, a bad deed. It is the lure of the woman, the wickedness of the woman, the seduction or the trickery of the woman who undoes the man. Or, it is her ineptitude that makes her the perfect victim and therefore, her fault. Either way, the woman is a victim of assault, and is then villainized.

Just as we can no longer hold onto the notion of what a bad guy looks like, we must change the way we see a victim.

When asked to describe a "victim," a high school group depicted a victim as "frail," "weak," "old" and, across the board for all male participants, "female." Sixty percent of the female respondents also envisioned a female as a victim. When the word "sexual" was attached to the word "victim," descriptions changed to include a female who is "young," "pretty," "sweet," and "helpless."

What is a Victim?

1. A victim is a person hurt or killed by someone or something by means of crime, accident, disaster, or disease.
2. A victim is a person (or animal) adversely affected by an action or circumstance.
3. A victim is someone duped, tricked, exploited.

Victims are not gender specific. In fact, almost 80% of all homicides are males with 23% being female. Of female homicide victims, however, the likelihood of being murdered by someone she knew was significantly higher.[11] Males, particularly those between teen and early twenties, are most likely to be victims of assault and robbery. Those living at poverty level (household incomes less than $12,000) have much higher instances of becoming victims of a violent crime while the middle-class have a higher percentage of experiencing property damage and/or theft. Blacks are more likely to be victims of violence than whites, and senior citizens are rapidly becoming the most targeted victims of online identity theft and mail fraud.[12]

Again, what does a victim look like?

In self-defense, however, our victims are predominantly female (though the number of males being the victims of assault by a partner or family members is on the rise). Despite what you see in the movies, the female is not always the human Barbie doll running on stilettos. Because predators are opportunists, they are more interested in finding a victim who is accessible and will not fight. Despite what the romance novels and movies suggest, victims of sexual assault come in all shapes and sizes, ages, demographics, and economic status. Predators are opportunists. Just like we cannot draw a picture of a bad guy, there is not specific image of a victim.

In Self-Defense:
There are two kinds of victims:
1. Victim of a stranger
2. Victim of a known associate like a family member, friend, neighbor, teacher, classmate, friend of a friend, employer/employee, etc.

Scenario #4: Is this My Fault?
You have been given the exciting opportunity to interview for a dream job or intern with a well-known professor or possibly join a dance squad. Upon meeting the person in power, you put out a hand to introduce yourself when he takes it, pulls you in and gives you a kiss on the cheek or even mouth. The grip on the hand is a little too hard and the hold is a little too long. Never mind – he just kissed you! You are stunned and embarrassed as you almost fell into him. He laughs at your clumsiness and you are instantly awkward and apologetic.

In this real-life scenario, a woman was allegedly greeted by a business mogul outside his private elevator. He took her hand for the shake but did not let it go. Then, he pulled her in for a kiss on the cheek and mouth, leaving her feeling "insignificant that he would do that."[13]

What Should She Have Done?

There can be no victim blaming here. Perhaps the woman needed this job opportunity to keep her home, pay medical bills, or pay off a loan. Who knows. The best response, however, would have been to end the meeting. There is no possibly way her assailant would ever give proper respect to her following this encounter and, most likely, the assaults would continue.

What Would You Do?

Let's come back to this. Read on.

Scenario #5: Is This My Fault?

You made the soccer team. You made the final cut in a casting call. You got a call back for a second interview for a great job. Whatever the scenario, becoming a victim is the very last thing on your mind. The only thing you care about and are thinking about is your competition or employment opportunity. And then it happens… You feel the eyes of your assailant looking you up and down in a way that is not flattering, professional, appropriate, or respectful. You feel yourself being appraised for your physical assets and you are revolted.

In this real-life scenario, women from the Miss USA pageant were told they would be personally inspected by Donald Trump. Reportedly, he would step in front of each contestant, look her up and down for inspection pre-contest. One contestant described it as "the dirtiest I've ever felt in my entire life,"[14] and she was left feeling demoralized, like "a piece of meat."

What Should She Have Done?

Victim Blaming Alert! For many, the first response to the beauty contestant being ogled is to say, *This is what she asked for. Isn't this what a beauty pageant is about?* Answer: No. While true the contest is about being judged on beauty, it is not about allowing a non-judge to line up *his* chattel, standing entirely too close to the women for an inspection they already passed by being accepted into the contest.

But now comes the question of what she and the rest of her competitors should have done. The situation is complicated by the fact a beauty contest that measures your worth by a beauty standard to be judged by others. While pageants offer many scholarships and great opportunities, it can be a slippery and dangerous slope in terms of self-worth, self-esteem and value as a person. You must have standards and safety precautions set in place and do not deviate from what is acceptable treatment and what is not. In this scenario, media exposure and complaints to sponsors of the event can help protect contestants from abuse within the pageant. The fact that this behavior continued so long proves only that no one was willing to speak out against the "authority" of the owner.

What Would You Have Done?

Rather than judge the girls and women in this scenario for being in a beauty contest, truly imagine how you would have reacted as the true issue here is what would you do in a scenario in which you felt violated by the person in power?

Scenario #6: Is This My Fault?

Despite being in a public setting, someone grabs and squeezes your buttocks. You are standing in a crowded room, on a bus or at a train station, you are with a group of friends or about to walk out on to a stage when this happens. This is an assault. Someone grabbing and squeezing your bottom is a sexual advance and an assault upon your person.

In this real-life scenario, a model and former Miss Finland was backstage at the Late Night with David Letterman Show when she was allegedly assaulted by Donald Trump. The act of aggression was so fast she had to wonder if it had actually happened.

What Should She Have Done?

In all three scenarios, the women were blindsided. In all three situations, a person of authority was the predator. In such events, the victim is uncertain how to move forward when the person they looked to for guidance was the aggressor. But imagine, if you will, if Miss Finland had whirled around and yelled, "Get your hands off of me!" before an entire studio audience? How many witnesses would have forever recalled that event and no matter whose side they chose to take, would have made note of the look of shock and embarrassment on the face of the aggressor.

In the far more private case of the elevator, had the woman pulled back and said, "What do you think you're doing?" the aggressor would have most likely laughed it off or, more probably, left her standing at the elevator – no job opportunity, no money. Witnesses complicate deniability. Without, it becomes one word against another. Staying mute, however, cannot be the answer. A person of authority who uses this position to assault another person does not have empathy for his victim. He will do it again and, you can bet, has done it many times before.

What Would You Do?

Re-Define Victim
Re-define Self-Worth

5
THE CASE OF BROCK TURNER

On January 18, 2015, an unidentified woman whom we will call "Jen" attended a fraternity party and drank so much alcohol that she lost consciousness while walking home.

By her own admission, she drank too much.
By her own admission, she wishes she had not.
By her own admission, she does not know how it came to be that she was assaulted.

What happened following her blackout Jen only knows through witnesses and forensic reports. She was so drunk that she did not wake up for many hours after the attack. What is known is that Jen was naked when two graduate students from Stanford University happened by on their bicycles. They saw Brock Turner, a stand-out swimming athlete with Stanford University on top of Jen, "aggressively thrusting his hips into her," said witness Carl-Fredrick Arndt. "The guy [Brock Turner] stood up, then we saw that she wasn't moving still. So we called him out on it. And the guy ran away, my friend, Peter, chased after him."

Turner claimed the sex, with Jen lying naked on the ground next to a dumpster, was consensual despite her blood alcohol level reportedly so high that she was rendered comatose for hours. When the case went to court, Turner's lawyer repeatedly urged the jury that "the only one we can believe is Brock, because she doesn't remember." The victim on trial was Brock Turner. Just before his sentencing, Turner's father appealed to the judge in a letter saying, "His [Brock] life will never be the one that he dreamed about and worked so hard to achieve. That is a steep price to pay for 20 minutes out of his 20 plus years of life."

Friends and family members of an aggressor never want to call a rapist a rapist, any more than they want to identify the deed as an assault. For Brock Turner's family, his assault on Jen was "20 minutes out of his 20 plus years of life," just as other aggressors explain that after they were caught (in person or on tape) pinching, kissing, pinning against a wall, grabbing a woman by her genitalia, abusing, coercing, or otherwise assaulting a woman that "that wasn't me. I'm not *that* person."

In turn, the victim spoke out by way of letter to the judge before a sentence was given. While Brock Turner's *tormented* 20 minutes altered his life, Jen wrote [to her assailant]:

"You took away my worth, my privacy, my energy, my time, my safety, my intimacy, my confidence, my own voice, until today. ... I don't want my body anymore. I was terrified of it," she wrote. "My independence, natural joy, gentleness, and steady lifestyle I had been enjoying became distorted beyond recognition. I became closed off, angry, self-deprecating, tired, irritable, empty," she said.[15]

Shortly after, Brock Turner was given a six month sentence, serving only three months when the standard punishment would have been up to 10 to 14 years in prison. For many more, this was a case of entitlement as well. Statistics show that male predators of a lower economic standing are far more likely to be imprisoned while upper-class white males walk or receive a slap on the wrist. Such was the case in the Brock Turner trial.

This case, in of itself, was not extreme. Sadly, there have been stories like this and worse throughout history. Women, drunk or sober, at night or in the morning, walking the streets or going for an early morning jog, alone with her thoughts or out with friends have been assaulted and then, for reasons that have everything to do with politics, sports, business, religion, prominence or denial, the woman's behaviors are questioned while the assailant(s) walk free. *He's not that kind of guy.* But she is forever a victim of his actions. *He didn't mean to do it.* But she is forever scarred by his deeds. His twenty minutes is her lifetime.

But it is here that you must define and re-define (again) the word "victim."

Are you a victim?

Will you be a victim?

What have you done to prepare yourself against this

probability?

If one in every five American women is assaulted at some point in her life, what are you doing to protect yourself?

Let's talk about that.

6
YOU DEFYING THE ODDS

Every 98 seconds, an American is sexually assaulted. Yet only 6 out of every 1,000 sexual predators will end up in prison. Currently, more than 90 women have lodged complaints of sexual assault against Harvey Weinstein. Former judge Roy Moore, Donald Trump, former NBC anchor Matt Lauer, comedian Bill Cosby, and talking head Bill O'Reilly have tallied a combined number of complaints well over 100. If the allegations are true, there are more than 200 victims attached to these six men. While there have been plenty of backroom settlements, it is unlikely any of the men will serve time for their alleged crimes of sexual assault.

With such astonishing statistics, why don't more women take self-defense classes to become more self-aware?

Why Don't More Women Take Self-Defense?
The main reasons given as to why women do not take self-defense classes are:

- I'm too old and/or out of shape.
- The idea of self-defense and someone pretending to come at me is scary.
- It's not realistic, and it won't work.
- I don't need self-defense; I have a gun.
- I want to, but I really can't afford it.
- I want to, but I don't want to do it alone.
- I don't want to get hurt.

Oh, You're Going to Get Hurt.
Let's start with this one:

If you are assaulted, you will be hurt.

If you fight back to save your own life, you will be hurt. If you do not fight, the probability of being beaten, punched, or worse is high. A sexual assault, without a punch, is violent and terrible. And only then do we begin to talk about the emotional pain and agony of the assault.

Just as you have been asked to define what "victim," "self-esteem," and "bad guy" are in your mind, you need to define "injury" because the long-term effects of rape are far worse than the average person understands.

It is remarkable and incredible and mind-blowingly astonishing how many people do not seem to understand this about sexual assault. When they question why a person did not immediately announce to the world that they were a victim of physical, mental, and emotional rape ("Why didn't you talk about this before?"), they exhibit a lack of understanding about what sexual assault truly is. It is not "20 minutes" of a person's life. It is not one terrible moment, followed by a hospital visit and one police report. It can be years and years of therapy and distrust; years and years of fear combined with emotional and physical scars; years and years of sleep interrupted with nightmares and flashbacks, hearing noises and growing paranoid; years and years of insecurities, self-doubt, guilt and self-loathing. Smells can ignite a painful flashback. The sound of a voice or the certain phrase can undo years of recovery. That *20 minutes* can be that harmful.

Oh, you will get hurt.

Does this scare you?

Please do not read these statements as a threat or scare-tactic but understand the message as it is intended. Sexual assault is a multi-layered horror show that features real pain and agony with a very real predator and a lingering affect that molds you – in one way or another. Each time the victim of a sexual assault hears of a politician or business mogul or athlete who assaulted another person (and, worse, walks away without punishment), it is a personal and private hell of reliving her own experience. Each time a person asks (born of ignorance) why the victim did not speak up earlier, blame is placed yet again on the victim.

Do not ask, "Will I be hurt?" but tell yourself, "I will survive." This is why you must learn to stand up for yourself – both physically and emotionally.

One of These Days … I'll Do It. One of These Days …

I'm Not in Proper Physical Condition

For the women who believe they are not in the required physical conditioning to defend themselves and thus do not take a self-defense class, they are already in great jeopardy. As you will later read, this is exactly the kind of mindset a predator looks for. Predators want an easy mark. They need a victim who can be easily bullied, frightened, and directed. *"Shut up or I will hurt you." "Don't move or I will …"*

It is important to know that much of self-defense has nothing to do with your fitness level. You don't have to be a fitness enthusiast, a weight lifter, or fighter to empower yourself. As you will later read, your attitude and voice are your most powerful weapons. But never pass up an opportunity for self-defense training because of a lowered fitness level. You deserve to learn how to defend yourself.

Note: Fitness level is important. The stronger you are, the greater your chances of fighting. Additionally, predators do not want a prolonged fight on their hands and will often actively choose a weaker victim. Always try to increase your fitness level for a happier, healthier, more active and prolonged life.

I Don't Have the Time for Self Defense/I Don't Have the Money for Self Defense

Priority is an amazing thing.

Women sit for hours and spend billions (collectively) on hair, manicures, massages, make-up and specialized procedures but neglect the most important thing – their life.

In truth, too many organizations and businesses charge too much money for self-defense programs. Ideally, this should be a free service. If you look, however, you can find self-defense classes offered by police, local women's organizations and women's groups that are either free or charge only for the materials required in the class. Make it a girls' night out with a group of friends and do this at least four times a year.

It's Not Realistic ... It Won't Work

There are several ways to respond to this:

1. If you never learn self-defense, then your assessment that it will not work for you is correct.
2. Without discussing the physical techniques of self-defense, what you can learn from self-defense in terms of how to think, how to react, what safety measures to consider of how and where to walk and park, how to project, etc., is the mental training that can save your life and empower you.
3. Mental and emotional empowerment are incredible tools in self-defense.
4. You may be right.

Let's talk about #4:

You might be right. The self-defense class you sign up for may not be practical or realistic, and it is for this (and other) reasons that this book was created. It is a pet peeve of many, many martial artists and self-defense instructors when otherwise well-meaning and qualified male instructors teach self-defense to mainstream, everyday women, using techniques that require:

- Years of practice
- Greater strength/mobility for leverage
- Multiple steps to execute
- Larger and stronger hands to execute moves
- Greater height to properly execute

Self-defense for women should be size friendly. It should be fast, and the techniques should be easy to remember and simple in execution. In a moment of great surprise or shock, you should be able to recall and react with ease.

On a personal note, it is always concerning when I meet someone who is a black belt and earned this honor in under three years. A true black belt takes years to master. Martial arts has been watered down to a business money-making venture in many, many cases. If and when you decide to take self-defense classes, investigate who is teaching and learn more about their business practices. It is yet another reason why I do not like seeing self-defense as a money-making venture.

It is important to research different self-defense courses and the instructor! Do not be afraid to contact the instructor and ask him/her for their resume, personal background, and how they got into teaching self-defense. Ask for references and check them out!

If the instructor you are talking to tells you that he or she has "full-proof" techniques that allow you to disable or flip a person, be wary. No technique is full-proof. As instructors, we can only teach specific moves to students. There is no way to know what the situation will be that may require self-defense, and it is for this reason that your emotional and mental state are far more important than physical prowess.

The Idea of Self-Defense is Scary

Self-defense is a state of mind and being. You WANT to fight for your life and you should.

In the world of self-defense fighting, if you're fighting for more than 30 seconds, you're losing.

When and wherever you take self-defense, the techniques should be simple; the set-up and execution should allow you to step away quickly; the methods should be easy to remember. Even still, this is why it is recommended that you continue to take self-defense classes for the rest of your life. The idea is simple: You owe yourself this self-assurance and confidence. Your life is worth protecting. The only thing that is truly scary about self-defense is not knowing how to protect yourself.

I Don't Need Self-Defense; I Carry a Gun

Congratulations. You just said the #1 thing that causes every self-defense instructor and every victim to roll their eyes.

Understandably, this statement makes people feel better, but now let's talk about the real world.

Sadly, many law enforcement and security instructors make these same ridiculous utterances. In real life, however, the sexual predator does not announce him (or her) self. In real life, most victims never have time to retrieve a can of mace, a gun, a knife, a baton, or a cell phone to call for help. Most victims never see the attack coming.

There are many rosy depictions of women earning concealed handgun licenses with promises that gun ownership can reduce instances of rape. This is, in fact, wrong and negligent information to pass along to the public.[16][17][18]

In the scenario of a woman already holding her gun in hand as she watches her aggressor slowly approach, then, yes. A gun could help her escape harm. In real life, only 10 percent of rapes are committed by a complete stranger who the victim never saw coming. In most cases, the women are with a person they trust and their gun is nowhere near them. In most cases, the assault is a blindside attack, leaving no time to do anything but scream unless she has trained to defend herself. But in most cases, because of the suddenness of the assault, because of the shock and the surprise, because of the poor or nonexistent training in preparation of this moment and, as you will later read, because of the retractive responses of most women, she will simply fold, unable to even scream.

I'm being attacked.
I'm going to be killed.
I can't believe this is happening to me.

In sports, countless studies have been devoted to learning the inner psyche of the athlete to overcome negative self-talk. In business, in academics, in personal relationships, self-sabotage can be a deal breaker or ender. Can you imagine, however, in that single moment – one in which your life hangs in the balance of another person's humanity, civility, decency and compassion -- and you have no say in your own outcome? Can you fathom the horror of looking into the eyes of a monster and, with no ability to save your own life, you can only hope he will have mercy upon your soul?

Some of you can. For this, there can only be gratitude that you survived to read these words and acknowledgment given to the emotional journey of recovery you have been put upon. You never asked for this, but you can survive it. I am sorry but am also proud of you.

For those who have never been assaulted in any manner, I am truly so grateful that this is the case and hope this never changes. Reality can be harsh, however, and so I always urge all females to learn to fight for her own life.

Many women view self-defense and fighting as the same thing and, fearful of being hurt, shy away. In training, the motions are the same. In theory, they are quite different. In self-defense, you are not the aggressor. You are loving yourself. You are fighting for yourself. You are protecting yourself.

The truth is, most fights and assaults go to the ground. Women should learn how to fight/defend from their backs. An attack is fast, vicious and most self-defense classes do not and cannot teach reaction time or how to overcome panic in order to fight/escape in a one- or two-class event.

Because so many men do not understand the fears, hesitations, physical limitations and emotional roadblocks a woman experiences, they are not equipped to instruct women in self-defense. I know I will get a lot of blowback on this comment … But I don't care.

It is for this reason that taking self-defense cannot be a one-time deal. Learning to protect yourself is a never-ending job you should LOVE! You should be as faithful to self-defense training as you are to maintenance for your car, beauty treatments for your person, or checking on financial statements at your bank.

Remember this: Not one victim I have ever talked to really thought she would be attacked … and then she was.

7
REACTION AND INACTION

Men are reactive. In times of threat, women (as a stereotypical rule) tend to be inactive. Or retractive. We shrink inward. How often have you seen a male lash out at something that startles him while a female draws her hands inward and screams?

After 30 years in martial arts, I still jump when something startles me. I HATE being scared and will gasp (or scream – even worse) and THEN ponder the idea of pounding you. During my competitive years as a fighter, I was known as a "head hunter" and I mostly fought men. I was a mean fighter, fast and aggressive (I know you're not supposed to say such things about yourself but, in self-defense world, you better know what and who you are and be ready to bring it!), yet will fly out of my seat when something scares me. I am innately female and proud of who I am. I also know that I can fight -- mean and dirty.

Whether I teach my *"In Defense of Me"* self-defense seminar for a corporation, a private group or one-on-one, men and women are universally the same in their responses. I will call someone up from the audience to strangle me. There is a nervous giggle from the crowd. The male will ask me, "You're not going to hurt me, are you?" Once I assure him that I am not, the choke or simulated strangle is usually pretty strong. Women will, as they are pathetically attempting to choke me, apologize. It is great comedic relief for the audience but is always the same. My female attacker whispers in my ear, "Sorry!" even as I am yelling at her to choke me harder.

In training with male and female athletes, working with members of the gym or teaching my college students, males and females react differently to confrontation. As a general (albeit sweeping) rule, males bow up to confrontation. *What's your problem? You lookin' at me?* Females shrink back, avert eye contact, and hope to get the heck out of the threatening situation.

The following pages and chapters have been created from

years and years of training athletes, students, victims and survivors, both male and female, young and old. ***Trumping the Rape Culture & Sexual Assault*** was designed to have you think more about you; think more about your surroundings; think more about your personal weapons; think more about how you may be viewed by others; and think more about the value of your life.

Scenario #7: Aggressor Action/Victim Inaction
Note: This title seems to suggest placing blame on the victim. No blame. It is a reality you must consider.

You are on an airplane, in an elevator or in a secluded area that is semi-public when you are assaulted. Though you are in public, you feel trapped.

In this real-life scenario, a woman is seated in first-class on a flight when her seatmate lifts up the armrest and physically grabs first her breasts and then attempts to put a hand up the woman's skirt. The time frame of this event is important as it occurred in the early 1980s when the "shame" of such an assault would have been on the woman for her own action. She had been in coach when the flight attendant allegedly escorted her to the front to sit in first class. Her alleged assailant had requested her presence and the woman soon found herself in the clutches of a predator by (unwittingly) her own doing. Of the assault, the woman said, "I don't recall saying no; I don't recall saying stop," she said. "I don't recall saying anything. It was like a silent pantomime. I remember at one point looking over at the guy in the seat across the aisle, and his eyes were like bugging out of his head."[19]

What Should She Have Done
The woman eventually made her way back to her original seat in coach and was so "rattled" that she remained there until the plane had landed and everyone de-boarded, fearful of a second confrontation with her attacker. Imagine, however, if she had yelled, looked directly at the man whose eyes were 'bugging out' and said, "Help!" Most likely the man would have done something, if only to have called for a flight attendant. There would have been some kind of rescue and plenty of witnesses. Again, this is not a judgement on the victim as we are merely imagining the best reaction in this terrible situation.

What would you do?

Unlike the alleged witness to this account, we hope that today's fellow passengers would step in to help. But don't count on it. All too often, a person needs to hear a "help" before acting. Unfortunately, however, many women are simply too stunned and/or embarrassed to call for help. Our voice is a powerful weapon. Why don't we use it more often?

Predators do <u>not</u> want attention drawn to themselves or to their actions. What they want and need is to be in an isolated area so that if you were to fight or yell, no help would be available to you. More on that later. For the purpose of this section, however, let's pay attention to the predator who has become so confident and so seasoned in how he attacks (pushing women against a wall to force himself against her, pushing his tongue in her mouth) and who he chooses (a woman who appears to be so impressed by his position of authority or money or opportunities he might provide) that she will not fight back.

He has chosen you for a reason.

Your silence and cooperation, even if it is you in a frozen and muted position, are necessary.

What he cannot have is a screaming, very public tirade that brings about witnesses. Further, he cannot afford to have a wound of any kind that would indicate self-defense tactics were needed. These wounds of a battle can also be described as evidence.

Scenario #8: Aggressor Action/Victim Inaction

This can't be happening. This is my job! You are working your job and are among your own peers when a potential client grabs you. Not only are your co-workers present but so, too, is the client's own wife. Hardly able to believe what is happening, you do nothing.

Maybe this isn't what I think it is. Maybe I'm misinterpreting this ...

In reality, however, you quickly realize this is all too real. In this real-life scenario, a female reporter for *People* magazine was doing a story about the one-year wedding anniversary of a celebrity and his wife when she was cornered and assaulted by the celebrity during a tour of the man's lavish home. In this attack, only when the butler interceded to inform the man that his wife was coming, did the attack stop. Remarkably, this assault picked up where it left off following the conclusion of the interview.

What Should She Have Done?

Again, there is no finger-pointing here. The situation was as extreme as it was absurd. The reporter was doing her job, with co-workers (this account would later be corroborated by six different people) and the predator's wife present. Even the butler knew what was going on. Despite having witnesses, she would later face great scrutiny when she told her story because rather than fight to leave marks on his person and/or run, she simply did her job and the attacker went unscathed. As you will read later, her shock was real. Her reaction of no (physical) reaction was a physiological response to the sudden and unwanted attack and re-attack.

What Would You Do?

Would you risk losing your job? Would a fight be worth jeopardizing a million-dollar deal for your company? Would you be able to stand up to a multi-millionaire threatening a lawsuit for defamation of character?

More importantly, do you know for a fact that you would have been able to physically fight or speak up?

With the power of your voice also comes that inner-voice – that gut-feeling you have when you know something is not right. Yet, how often do women ignore the inner-voice because we have been trained to be nice, to not offend and be the good girl?

How often have you continued to talk to someone who gave you the creeps or walk down a hallway or street that made you uneasy, willfully ignoring all the bells and whistles going off in your mind?

How many times have you allowed a relationship to continue with a person you no longer wanted any part of because you did not want to hurt that person's feelings, despite the fact that this person truly did not care about what was best for you?

Scenario #9: Aggressor Action/Victim Inaction

You are having a wonderful time at an event and all eyes are on the game, the dance, the entertainer, or show when suddenly you feel something – a pinch or the slide of a hand. You realize that you are being molested.

It is a stunning revelation as you are in a crowd of people at this joyous event when something crude and offensive happens.

In this real-life scenario, a woman was attending an event in a public setting to watch legendary singer Ray Charles perform. She was acting as an assistant to the photographer at the event and suddenly found herself being molested by the event's host.

What Should She Have Done?

She told her friend what happened but mentioned the assault to no one else. At the time, while it was upsetting, her focus remained on her friend.

Had she known a decade later that evidence of this assault could have been crucial in identifying a serial sexual deviant, would she have reacted differently? In fact, in each of the previous scenarios, had these women known that their assault, subsequent testimony and need for witnesses could have feasibly changed the course of history, would they have been willing to be more aggressive in their protests?

Most likely, the answer would be a resounding "yes." Women are very good about looking after one another. But no one thinks this way in the moment of an attack. Laughably, the assertion has been made that these women are also somehow to blame for not getting evidence DURING their assaults, as if that was anywhere on their minds. There is no question that these women are very brave to come forward, but the shock had to wear off and the recovery had to begin before they could speak out.

Many women actually come forward after an assault not for themselves but for others. This is innately a female trait.

Why do we have to be pushed to serve others before we serve ourselves when it comes to something as egregious as sexual assault or harassment?

What Would You Do?

Your friend could likely lose the best paying gig of his professional career if you speak up. Do you? And are you so certain that the act that was forced upon you was so egregious that it would trump any lawsuit, denials, or public scrutiny? How much does that all matter to you? And who would stand with you in these more challenging times? Does that matter?

For women, for those who are more inclined to be inactive in defense of themselves, these are hard questions to answer. Yet, these are always the questions asked, are they not?

Historically speaking, powerful men with a lot of money and even more contacts are rarely punished when it comes to such matters. Already embarrassed, mad, violated and stunned, you can see why it seems much easier for the victimized women to walk away and tell no one.

8
REBEL YELL

When was the last time you roared like a lion?
No?
Never?

Let's experiment.

Go to a private area – your car, a closet, the bathroom and let rip. Yell (not scream, but yell), roar and rage, as though you were warning off a dangerous predator. Yell so fiercely that even a stampeding bull would stop short and reconsider you.

How did you sound?
Pathetic, right?
Now ask yourself, how is this sound you made possibly going to ward off any bad guys?

By age 20, most women have received their high school diploma or higher. Most women have earned a driver's license and most are registered voters. Most women have gone to a bank, opened an account, and have credit. Most women have a car and see to it that the oil is changed and the gas tank is full, yet far too few take any kind of self-defense course. This is despite increasing research that shows that women who partook in a self-defense training program were 98.3% more likely to avoid assaults all together.[20] More studies show that with at least 12 hours of training/education about safety, sexual assault and self-defense, 97% were able to fight off their attacker, and upward of 80% used the power of their voice and body language to thwart an assault.[21]

Dispelling the "I 'carry'; therefore, I am safe" myth:

As previously stated, the idea that carrying a gun in your purse or backpack will prevent a sexual attack is not only factually incorrect (despite serious efforts from gun enthusiasts to say otherwise), it is a dangerous myth.

Awareness

The #1 asset a person can have to help prevent a sexual assault is awareness. You have heard this statement a hundred times: *Be aware of your surroundings!* But how many times have you walked into a parking lot talking on the phone or sat in your car fiddling with makeup or been lost in deep thought in public? How often have you gone for a walk or gone jogging with the music turned up just a little too loudly? How often have you struggled to carry groceries from your car to the front door, barely aware of who is there, in your quest to limit your trips between the car and house?

We've all done it.

We tell ourselves that "be aware of your surroundings" is only necessary when in an unfamiliar place or when you get a creepy vibe from someone. Right?

Wrong. Self-awareness and situational awareness are a constant, never-ending aspect of survival and self-defense. In fact, most women are assaulted in a known, comfortable environment such as their home, the home of a friend, or the office, i.e., a place where their guard is down.

What is Self-Awareness?

Self-awareness is recognizing yourself as an individual in your environment (whatever and wherever that is) in the physical sense but also identifying your own traits, or your personality, to include your strengths and weaknesses, fears and beliefs, and how you respond to different situations. Self-awareness does not just include yourself but how you interact with other people and how they perceive and receive you. In self-defense, this self-awareness is how a predator may come to choose you as a victim. Though most aggressors are opportunists, they are (cowards, by nature) more apt to choose a victim who will not fight. How you present yourself (i.e. – how you see yourself) and how the world sees you (i.e. – how you present yourself) is critical in survival and self-defense.

What is Situational Awareness?

In self-defense, situational awareness is the here and the now. It is: 1) your current environment and situation

2) your comprehension of your current situation
3) your response to your current situation.

This is so important. Women who have never had any kind of self-defense or martial arts training tend to retract in threatening situations.

We look down and/or avoid eye contact with the perceived threat.

We turn our backs on the predator in an attempt to hurry away from the perceived threat.

We ignore natural instincts to call for help and use the "hope and pray" tactic to survive the situation.

In essence, most women ignore situational awareness cues, whereas most men do not.

Have you ever noticed how men instinctually do not like sitting in a public restaurant with their backs to the door? They like to sit on the outside of the aisle. The smallest man (in stature) bows up when he perceives a threat. Have you ever noticed how men will puff up the chest, pull the elbows outward and bring up the chin while walking in a crowd? Men react to their situational environment.

Instilling the "I roar; therefore, I am safe" tactic:
It's time to roar.

Again, it is time to practice both your actual and your metaphorical roar.

- Pay attention to your surroundings
- Keep your hands free. A distracted person makes for a great victim.
- Walk with confidence. Body language is everything. Chin up, back straight, eyes always scanning the crown, project an air of confidence.

The Story of Leigh Ann
Leigh Ann was doing everything right. She attended kickboxing classes twice a week, had taken self-defense classes, and was physically strong. But, like all of us, she had a moment of bad judgment. She was in the historic downtown Fort Worth

stockyards in Texas where she met up with some friends for a couple of hours. When she decided it was time to head back to her car, she took a short-cut through an alley. Then she realized that she had company behind her and quickened her pace but, it seemed, so did the man behind her. Panic flooded her thoughts.

As she tells the story, she thought about what she had learned in our kickbox and self-defense classes.

Your voice is your greatest weapon.

Use your voice.

Surprise your aggressor.

Have the upper hand.

Your voice is your greatest weapon.

She turned on him like a rabid dog, charging and barking. Yes. Barking.

The man halted, hands up. "Whoa!"

Then Leigh Ann turned and ran for her car. As she struggled, hands trembling, to get her car door open, the man emerged from the alley. He was coming toward her! At last, she was able to turn the lock and get into her car, watching the approaching man in her rear view mirror as she fumbled to get the key into the ignition. She readied herself for what was to come. Then, she said, "he got into the car behind me."

As she recounted this story to our kickboxing class, her classmates howled with laughter and Leigh Ann, a sheepish grin on her face, could only shake her head. "I was so embarrassed."

What Would You Do?

Be honest. Most women would have simply prayed that they were just being paranoid and hoped to make it out of the alley alive. A smaller population would have broken into a run. About two percent would have done as Leigh Ann did.

Genuinely ask yourself what you would have done. Would you have been able to turn, charge and bark?

What would you have done?

The bigger question is WHY would only two percent have done as Leigh Ann did? Why do so few women protect themselves? Why do so many "hope and pray" to make it out alive when all they have to do is turn, charge and bark?

It is such an easy thing to do. Turn. Charge. Bark.

Ahh.

Leigh Ann was wrong.

The guy was just a guy – not a predator. (She thinks.)

While her fellow classmates laughed at the story, they also applauded her.

Leigh Ann did the right thing.

That was awesome.

I'll bet that guy will think twice before following a woman so closely in a darkened alleyway.

Now you've got a great story to tell!

But there was something much more important about Leigh Ann's proactive charging and barking. While the above comments are all true, I made one thing abundantly clear to her classmates:

Leigh Ann found her Rebel Yell.

I was so proud of Leigh Ann's willingness to protect herself and creativity in shocking her presumed aggressor. But there was an important question to ask: "Would you be able to do that again?" Leigh Ann was adamant.

Yes!

Women and girls are so conditioned by cultural norms to be kind, patient, sweet and forgiving that it is to our own detriment. Can you imagine the scenario where a man aggressively assaults (sexually or physically) another man in a public setting and the man quietly frees himself and runs, only to whisper-tell other people? Chapter 12, "*Let's Hear It For the Boys*," discusses how often boys and men are victims of sexual assault – you'd be surprised – but public settings are far more rare. Why?

Men are supposed to fight.

Men are supposed to stand their ground.

Women are not supposed to raise their voices, cause a scene, or fight. Even in the online gaming world.

By 2012, the non-gaming world became aware of how violent video gamers are toward their female opponents. By 2016, more than 40 percent of gamers were female but the macho environment, depictions of buxom females and gaming-themes, all very anti-female, allowed for a culture in which very un-macho, stereotypical males who would typically be bullied by their own male peers in everyday life, made repeated threats against women. In the documentary *GTFO*, filmmaker Shannon Sun-Higginson reveals just how bad sexual harassment is against female gamers, and how extremely reluctant those female gamers are to complain for fear of losing their position (or ranking as a gamer) within the industry.[22] While a skilled male gamer may be called harmless names, most laden with comical yet respectful remarks, similarly skilled female gamers are met with something quite different and disturbing. The following remarks were directed to just one successful female gamer in just one example:

"@_____, I violently masturbated to your face on your latest video."

"@_____, I'll rape you and put your head on a stick …"

"@_____, suck' ma dick, u a slut"

"Why don't you kill yourself and make a video about it?"

"…the only place for women is in chains in my kitchen…"

"@_____, suck my cock and cook me a steak."

"Wouldn't it be funny if five guys raped her right now?"

"Why did the feminist cross the road … TO SUCK MY DICK."

"She needs a good dicking…"[23]

Even in the cyber world, even among some of the most stereotypically geeky men on earth, women are belittled and degraded as entertainment. The idea is simple: Bully and threaten until women leave and, if they stay, they must like it.

There is that long-held belief that women secretly like aggressive behavior in the way of sexual assault. As is told in the history of the rape of the Sabine women. According to lore, when the leader Romulus founded Rome in the 8th century, it was done so with mostly men. Facing a shortage of women (and new generations), Romulus concocted a plan to hold a festival and when the residents of Sabine, a neighboring tribe, arrived, the Romans would capture their women – only the virgins – and make them their wives. Later, when the Sabines regrouped and came back to claim their women, the non-virgins begged to stay for they now loved their Roman captors because that's how non-virgins think.

This plot would be used again in the movie, *Seven Brides for Seven Brothers*, when seven brothers steal women from their sleeping beds to make them their wives. Like the Sabine women, these soon-to-be-brides fall in love with their captors because that's how virgins think. Yeah. The movie was made in 1954 so it was important that the victims not be hussies so they remained virgins on the mountains until the preacher man came.

The point being that virgins and non-virgins alike should always be kidnapped when a man needs a wife.

In May of 2017, the United Nations conducted a survey in just four Middle Eastern countries (Egypt, Morocco, Lebanon, and Palestine) where the vast majority of men admitted to sexually harassing women in public, ranging from ogling and derogatory comments to sexual groping and rape because it was "fun." Of those men, 90 percent agreed that women who dressed provocatively deserved to be heckled and/or assaulted and that women like being sexually harassed as it is "positive attention."[24]

As long as the world stays mute on the issues of domestic abuse and honor killings (the killing of a female relative who is perceived to have brought dishonor on the family), sexual harassment and the degradation of females simply because they are females, these behaviors will persist worldwide. Our sisters in nations in the Middle East, Africa, and elsewhere that ignore the abuse of women are still OUR SISTERS. Their torment is our torment. And just because a woman is a victim of sexual assault in a nation that accepts such barbaric behaviors as the norm doesn't make it any less criminal or horrific.

The Lessons of Leigh Ann

Watching Leigh Ann retell the story of her alleged attacker is fun. As she reenacts that moment she realized her would-be "rapist" just wanted to get into his own car, she slumps with humiliation and every woman listening laughs with empathy.

But her embarrassment is also critical because it points to one of main reasons (if not the main reason) why women do not yell and scream when threatened. *What if we're wrong?*

But she was amazing.

She was brave.

She used her voice and protected her number one – Leigh Ann. And even as I said, "Boy, don't you know that guy will think twice about following a woman down an alley again," we all rolled with laughter because we knew it was true. *Ya did good, Leigh*

Ann. Ya did good.

In nations where women are daily subjected to violence and degradation in accordance to cultural norms, it is unfair to ask that they raise their voices – though we can hope. For women in western and, supposedly more advanced, nations where women's rights are concerned, it is always unfair to judge how one woman responds to her own personal assault. As a people, however, as a collective group, we can help each other find our voices. But it starts today with just one – yours.

Don't Just Speak Up – Roar!

This is it: You're being attacked. It is not just about yelling. It is about making your assailant think.

Remember this … the act of aggression is NOT about you. It has nothing to do with your beauty or charm. This is a power trip through violence and degradation. You need to speak to your assailant in a manner he can understand. As this assault, this crime is about his own power trip, remind him of what HE has to lose. If you are in a public setting, remind him:

- "I just called 911."
- "You don't want to do this. There are multiple witnesses."
- "Ever heard of technology? There are literally seven cameras surrounding us. Every angle of this assault is being recorded."

Particularly when the assailant knows his victim (and visa versa), there is often too much to lose in this scenario. Be prepared for the fact that he will call you "bitch," "tease," "instigator," and claim you misled him, but the idea is to make him think about long-term repercussions for him.

In a setting that is still public but the assailant is a stranger, the advantage is still yours as you ARE in public and can use modern technology (aka – evidence) in your favor. If, however, you are in a remote, more secluded area and not even your rebel yell can illicit outside help, your demeanor can still command attention. Rather than beg or cry, which does not work, commence to vulgar, loud threats, bad language, and the promise of horrible things AS you are getting ready for the fight of your life.

Be the exact opposite of what your assailant wanted.
Defend you.
Fight for you.

Go practice your roar.

9
THE DON'T-MESS-WITH-ME-WALK

In my "In Defense of Me" self-defense seminars, there are four major points to the lecture:

- Listen to and respect your inner voice.
- Roar – the rebel's yell.
- Walk the Don't-Mess-with-Me walk.
- Game on!

Make no mistake: The roar (both literal and figurative) is important. But do not forget that aggressors are opportunistic. They do not choose victims they believe will roar mightily in public any more than they choose a victim who could kick their ass.

Frank but true.

They look for someone who looks uncertain, afraid to fight back, afraid to speak up, unable (or unwilling) to roar. In the corporate, sports, academic, literary, healthcare, entertainment, restaurant, and hospitality worlds, to name but a few, aggressors will also look for someone who has a horse in the race. That is, they look for someone who is afraid to speak out for fear of losing a job, a promotion, a title, a position, a grade, or a review. They look for women who can be silenced through intimidation.

There is no greater example of this than Donald Trump's ownership of beauty pageants. From 1996 to 2015, Trump owned the Miss Universe Organization, including Miss USA and Miss Teen USA, until he was forced to sell in 2015. During that time, there were multiple complaints of Trump walking into the dressing rooms of beauty queens as they changed clothing, including many repeated walk-ins on Miss Teen contestants. In 2005, Trump even bragged while on the *Howard Stern Show* that he would walk in while women and girls were getting dressed, saying, "You know, no men are anywhere. And I'm allowed to go in because I'm the owner of the pageant. And therefore I'm inspecting it... 'Is everyone okay?' You know, they're standing there with no clothes. 'Is everyone okay?' And you see these incredible-looking women, and so, I sort of get away with things like that."[25]

The complaints about inappropriate hugging, kissing on the lips, public degrading, and frequent appearances back stage while contestants were naked or half-naked were plentiful but there appeared to be no stopping Trump as he was the owner and, in bragging about his lascivious behaviors, was emboldened by his own power. Only when Jill Harth, a former business partner of Trump, sued him for attempted rape in the bedroom of his daughter, Ivanka, did Trump settle out of court for an undisclosed sum of money, but it did not change his own patterns of behavior. He settled out of court, but he was not criminally punished.

It is very important to note that aside from the Brock Turner and Leigh Ann stories, all of the other real-life examples in this book of alleged assaults were perpetrated by the same man – Donald Trump, a known (by his own admissions) aggressor and sexual predator. When we do not speak up, those who attack will attack again. And again. And again. And with each assault and the continued degradation of our fellow sisters, such monsters grow in confidence, insulting females leaders, entrepreneurs, educators and pioneers for being strong, independent, and smart – all things that aggressors do not like in a female.

Walk Tall

The expression "Walk tall" means to walk with an air of confidence and self-assurance, to have pride in oneself and pride in one's own actions.

This is it.

There is no magic equation here, no tricks for which you need to pay hundreds of dollars to look menacing and ward off bad guys. Take everything you have read and apply it to your walk. Here goes:

- Be aware of your surroundings.
- Stay off the cell phone while in public.
- Make mental notes of who you pass, how they approach you, and keep a respectful distance from those you do not

know or who might give off a bad vibe.
- May eye contact.
- Walk tall – head up, face the world, shoulders squared, exuding confidence.

Easier said than done?

No. For the most shy and/or insecure person, practice can make for a taller walk! Just as you need to practice your yell, you can practice how you walk and how you are perceived.

Practice Confidence
- Start with a "hello." As you pass people, say, "hi." For shy people, this is a difficult task but it is empowering. As you do this more and more, you will notice how many people do not make eye contact. You're in control with the "hello." But it also ensures that you know what people look like. You are aware. You are personally and situationally aware!
- Strong Spine. Did you know that when you drop your head to read your text messages (the average adult head weighs between 10 to 12 pounds), upwards of 60 pounds of pressure pulls on the spine. With the average American sending/receiving 128 texts per day, imagine how much this changes the individual spine and how we stand. Pinch your shoulders back, lift your chin and just watch how differently people look at you. You are walking tall.
- Adopt a mantra. Whether you tell yourself you are brave or strong, you are loved or needed, remind yourself of your worth. You are entitled to respect, courtesy, and safety.

Continue to Grow Your Confidence
- Stay Self-Aware: Always know where you are going, who you will be with, and who may be watching you.
- Recognize your weaknesses and create an on-going list on how you might improve them. For example, if you are weak in strength, find the resolve to get in better shape.

Learn to box. Learn to fight. Make new friends in doing this. If you are shy, joining a fitness class just might break you out of your comfort zone. If you are unable to do these things due to physical limitations, empower yourself in different ways: Be sure to have a call button you can always press or an open line on the phone and tell your phone friend, "Yup, I'm passing a guy who looks like .." "Oh, and now I'm on 73rd Street and ..." but be sure you are not distracted by chitchat. Have these "safety calls" be all about your own personal safety.

- Recognize your strengths and capitalize on them. Make your presence and persona strong. If you are in a wheelchair or use a walker, your presence is still strong with a strong voice, a steely gaze, and an open phone line!
- Believe in yourself. Practice your own private mantra until you believe what you are saying. You are your own #1.
- Do not be afraid of being hurt. If you are chosen to be a victim ... you WILL be hurt. Be prepared to fight for yourself. Repeat: You are your own #1.
- Know that it is okay to be scared or feel threatened, but you must still stand up for yourself. You must still roar.

The Art of Eye Contact
& the Art of War Games

In developing your confidence as you walk, you are also developing new situational awareness skills that could save your life. For many, however, making eye contact is so intimidating that most do not do it and, despite knowing better, continue to walk with eyes downcast.

So, play a game:

Identify Features. Every day, identify a different feature (physical or one of attitude) in people and count how many you see each time you are on public streets, taking public transportation, or jogging along a quiet path. Count how many times you see someone with a mustache, wearing mirrored sunglasses, walking with an altered gait (a limp, a stoop, etc), or wearing boots. In doing so, you are always scanning the horizon. Fixate on a number.

As you jog, you want to see five dogs, seven people wearing earbuds, and five people wearing hats. On the metro, you want to see nine people wearing Reeboks, four people reading a book, 10 people talking on their phones, and seven people wearing a gold chain.

Actively make yourself look for different characteristics and/or physical descriptions. In doing so, you WILL make eye contact with people, you will be aware of the movement of people and, most importantly, you will appear more confident, alert and less suitable to be a victim.

Make no mistake: The rape culture as well as the blame culture are a war on women. The idea that every 98 seconds an American is sexually assaulted yet only six out of every 1,000 sexual predators will end up in prison is appalling. That a successful businessman can repeatedly assault women, brag about it, yet never face any punishment is a battle cry for justice.

So prevalent is the rape culture that the overwhelming majority of assaults are perpetrated by someone the victim knows. The attacker relies on the victim remaining a victim – not reporting it, not fighting back, not telling anyone.

Developing your confidence means developing your self-worth and self-esteem. It means learning to walk tall, use your voice, and listen to that inner-voice telling you that something (or someone) is wrong. It means redefining the word "victim" because it is not or will no longer be you.

This is war and you're going to win.

10
LOCKER ROOM TALK ISN'T
JUST TALK

When the audio of the "Access Hollywood" tape was released, sharing with the world how objectifies and assaults women, Trump's response was not to seek professional counseling or acknowledge his many victims but to write it off as locker room talk.

Oh, whew.

It was just locker room talk.

The insulting, demeaning, violent talk about attacking women and admitting that his star power allowed him to pursue this aggressive behavior was just locker room talk.

A president of any nation serves as a role model and is called upon for diplomacy, yet this one is known for his aggressive behavior against women. *But it was just locker room talk. Nothing wrong here – just locker room talk.*

In a national study of 10,000 K-12 teachers, counselors, and administrators, 90 percent said there was a negative impact following the presidential election in November 2016. In what has become known as the "Trump Effect," educators reported skyrocketing incidents of bullying, harassment and targeting of students, in particular, girls, disabled and/or special needs, immigrants, or LGBT. In yet another study conducted by the Human Rights Campaign, a non-profit for the betterment of all people, 50,000 students between the ages of 13-18 were polled. The study, believed to be the largest ever of its kind, highlighted the Trump Effect. Seventy percent of the responding teenagers personally witnessed acts of aggression and bullying during and since the election.[26][27][28]

The act or talk of physically assaulting women is never okay, and politics is not the only place where such behaviors take place. In locker rooms (literally) across the nation, there is a rise in violent and degrading attitudes about girls/women in high school, collegiate and professional locker rooms. Particularly with college and professional athletes, victims are publicly disgraced, even threatened, to drop any charges against athletes as play time equals money, humanity be damned. In a study of male student athletes, who only comprise of three percent of the student population, were found to commit 19 percent of sexual assaults and 35 percent of domestic assaults in a study conducted in the 1990s.[29]

Historically speaking, universities and colleges provide support to the student athlete accused of rape while completely neglecting the victim. Most rapists are repeat offenders, statistically averaging six rapes before they are caught. If they are caught.[30]

"Sexual Coercion Practices Among Undergraduate Male Recreational Athletes, Intercollegiate Athletes, and Non-Athletes" published in Violence Against Women in 2016 concluded that 54 percent of college student athletes are involved in some form of sexual coercion.[31]

While men in power are not only <u>not</u> held accountable for their actions but often protected against punishment, there is impact among our youth – particularly young males who see any form of privilege or position of authority as a means to demean others and get away with it. So how do we end the cycle of violence if it continuously churns?

Locker Room – Board Room – Classroom Talk
If we accept that males are allowed to disrespect, disparage, and dishonor females as long as it is funny (to them), the problem persists. For those who find humor in the insults and sexual references or who share a chuckle with teammates or co-workers, they argue the demeaning remarks are harmless and the rest of us need to get over it.

Even for the men who know better and don't especially like locker room talk, studies show that the majority of males go along with it for fear of being considered less manly by peers.[32]

Why Locker Room Erodes Society
But peer pressure does not excuse the talk. If you're not part of the solution, you're part of the problem.

Each time a person ignores locker room talk, the silence is acceptance to those perpetuating the belief that women are not of equal standing and/or importance to men. When someone (or even something) is continuously diminished overtime, she or he (or it) loses value.

How Do We Stop This?

In asking the question, "How do we stop this?", there must first be more questions asked:

- How many times has a 12- or 13-year-old girl, upon developing breasts, suddenly become aware of an adult male staring at (sometimes commenting about) her new changing body in a way that makes her feel uncomfortable, embarrassed, even ashamed?
- How many times in a woman's lifetime will she hear, "just a girl," "fights like a girl," "screams like a girl," "acts like a girl," etc., in the form of an insult to other males?
- How often is a female assault victim judged by what she was wearing, what company she kept, how sober (or not) she was, how she behaved rather than having all judgement focused on the attacker?
- How many times after a girl or woman politely declines an unwanted approach from a male does she suddenly find herself being called names and/or harassed for simply saying "no"?
- How many times, every day, do women ignore inappropriate comments from complete strangers, co-workers, even neighbors and friends because we're supposed to be nice?
- How many times have you been told to "get over it?" and you did – just to be a good girl?
- How betrayed have you felt knowing fellow neighbors and colleagues deem a predator suitable to "lead" because his crimes were "only" perpetuated against "a girl"?

Better yet, share these questions with other men and women. When we create more dialogue about these issues, we can make change. And there can be no greater time, for we have now seen that our fellow neighbors will choose a monster over humanity for their party line. But we have other issues brewing which are a direct result of the locker room talk/Trump effect. The rising and most shocking demographic for online pornography viewing in recent years is girls under the age of 12. Think about this:

- 12% of all websites on the internet are pornographic.
- 40 million Americans regularly view pornography.
- Annually, internet pornography makes $4.9 billion worldwide. The U.S. pornography draws $2.84, over half of the world's earnings.
- 2.5 billion emails per day are pornographic.
- 20% of men admit they view pornography while at work.[33]

With the prevalence of "just" locker room talk comes an unconscious attitude that everyone adopts. It is okay to joke about rape and how a man wants to "wreck" a woman and it is acceptable to minimize the value of a female. Long term, when females are "just" a girl, over-reactive, emotional, it is also easier (as has been historically demonstrated) for law enforcement, prosecutors, judges, civil servants, and juries to dismiss claims of sexual harassment and/or abuse. As we saw in the state of Alabama, millions of citizens were willing to put a suspected child molester and sexual predator in office rather than vote against their party line because said victims were "just" girls and "why did they wait so long to speak out?"

Despite dozens and dozens of eyewitness accounts to Judge Roy Moore's alleged predatory behaviors, including those who happened to be police officers and city employees, millions decided a suspected predator was okay. Locker room talk and its macho attitude degrades other humans as well as society.

And this pathetic banter does not remain only in locker rooms.t is also in board rooms and classrooms. It is in businesses and homes, in hospitals and in the White House.

So do we get over it, or fight it?

Your call.

11
THE GIRLS CLUB:
EVERYONE WELCOME

Just as dangerous as the "just a girl" and "just locker room talk" mentalities is the statement, "You know how women are ..."
You know how it is when you get a group of women together. Women are just mean.

Study Shows Women are Meaner

A 2011 study, authored by a University of Ottowa professor and reported in the psychology journal *Aggressive Behavior*, claims that women are genetically predisposed to bitchy behavior. The behaviors of 86 Canadian women were studied after a younger and sexier subject entered the research room. When the young and sexy subject was dressed conservatively, the controls (the 86 women) largely ignored her. However, when the young and sexy subject wore a tight skirt and revealing shirt, 97 percent of the women reacted "inappropriately" on a "bitchy-behavior scale" of zero to 10.[34]

Where, however, is the counter study? Where is the study that introduces a sexy, hot, young male dressed in his Magic Mike costume entering the room full of conservatively dressed males?

This isn't one.

There isn't one because there is no belief that men would display inappropriately "bitchy" behaviors. But, of course, we know this is not true. The reality is people are people. Those with lower self-esteem will find fault with and judge others based on appearance, behaviors and/or material items, regardless of gender.[35]

New Study Shows ...

But wait! The same psychology journal, *Aggressive Behavior*, subsequently released a 2014 study conducted by the University of Georgia that, in fact, boys are meaner than girls. This study included 620 students, not collected into one room but randomly chosen from six different school districts from grades 6 to 12. Based on passive and physical aggression, boys are meaner than girls, not just through physical aggression but also through spreading rumors and excluding and rejecting their classmates.[36]

But wait! Yet another study published in the *Nature Human Behavior* journal in 2017 revealed research from the University of Zurich that women's brains (biology) makes females kinder, gentler, more tolerant and accepting, more giving and better caregivers than men.[37]

There is no doubt that our youth and beauty obsessed culture creates friction among women. Many a petty woman has done and said things she ought not have. But to say that women are "meaner" is false.

Man-Bashing

All of this is not to say women are better than men. People are people. This is not man-bashing information.

And there it is...

You read that, right?

The qualifier.

The explanation.

The truth about women that ultimately showed we're pretty great people followed by the quick de-fuser "but we're not man-bashing."

Why is this needed?

Do we not hear every day, day after day, how horridly women treat each other, that women are petty and catty, that women are materialistic, that we cannot get along with each other; we are vain and weak and perpetually problematic?

But that is not considered woman-bashing; that's "just how women are."

Now THIS is a man-bash: At no time in history has a woman been stranded alone on a mountain top or in the desert or in the woods and stumbled upon a goat and said to herself, "Welllll, heyyyyy there," and raped the goat. Yet, historically speaking, it has NEVER been good for a wayward forest creature or mountain dwelling animal to stumble upon a lonely man. But I digress.

Woman-Bashing: And the Queen Bee Syndrome

The term "Queen Bee" was conjured by social psychologist Graham L. Staines and two colleagues in a *Psychology Today* article printed in 1974. Staines hypothesized that successful women opposed the women's liberation movement, enjoying their own successes as the "queen bee."[38]

Just as history, written by men, has long depicted women as spiteful, vengeful and mean, the Queen Bee Syndrome seemed to legitimize all previous claims, emphasizing some stereotypes as natural traits of women. The successful woman exhibits more masculine traits while the vulnerable woman is hormonal, according to the Queen Bee Syndrome. Like the Canadian study sampling 86 women, there is no balance here. A man feels grumpy, has a bad day or is just being an ass, but he's still a man. A woman feels grumpy, has a bad day or is being an ass, and she's "on the rag," "hormonal," "PMS-ing," and is a bitch.

Unfair? You bet.

How do we stop this?

We just do.

We can't ask that this double standard trash talk stop with men and expect the results we want. It must start with us. Stop accepting negative talk about other women. Rather, praise your sisters and remind all who will listen how much women balance out the world.

We must be more proactive in how women are portrayed, treated, and respected in our own communities.

Women vs. Women

- Stop repeating expressions that are demeaning to women, such as You know how women are." YOU are a female. Stop demeaning yourself! If your friend is being an ass, she's being an ass, and this has nothing to do with being a female.
- Recognize that men engage in indirect aggressive behaviors like gossiping and social exclusion just as frequently as women. In fact, studies have shown that men are worse.[39]
- Stop negative female speak when you hear it.

- Recognize that media images promote a woman's worth through being slender, sexy, and vulnerable. Stop allowing and/or endorsing this depiction. Refuse music, movies, TV shows, and books where women are perpetual victims without a voice and without justice.

Beware of the "All My Friends Are Guys" Gal

You know who she is. She's all in. She's completely cashed into the idea of being liked by men by throwing her own kind under the bus. She's the one who tells anyone who will listen that women are catty, backstabbing, and boring. She'll claim that guys are more fun and more real.

Why All this Girl Talk?

It's time to shift gears. Stop talking about how you want and need to lose weight, how your friend's metabolism is unfairly fast, how you wish you were taller or shorter, fitter or faster. Stop talking about that "bitch" in the office next to yours or down the hall and focus on the positive. Focus on the positives of women as a whole.

- We are a powerful voting bloc.
- We are the world's leading consumers.
- Today's American women over the age of 50 are the healthiest, wealthiest and most active generation of women in history.
- In the next decade, women will control two thirds of consumer wealth in the U.S. and are slated to be the beneficiaries of the largest transference of wealth in U.S. history.
- Wealthy female investors have officially outnumbered (doubling) their male counterparts in the U.S. [40]
- Women have exceeded men in earning both undergraduate and graduate degrees from college.
- Women are now the majority in the U.S. workforce.
- Women hold over half of managerial positions in the U.S. workforce.
- Worldwide, women's leadership and political

participation has risen to an all-time high.

- With women entering into political decision-making processes, quality of life for women promises to be on the rise.[41]
- Globally, women have demonstrated the proven ability to work across party lines through parliamentary women's caucuses, even within the most politically combative environments. [42]

In short, we freaking rock.

But what does this all have to do with self-defense, self-awareness, trumping your attacker, and changing how we view (and treat) women?

Everything.

Absolutely everything.

When we accept and acknowledge that we are powerful leaders and innovators; that we are changing the political landscape; and influencing business, marketing and laws, we can stop accepting the bullshit that has been spoon-fed to us since birth.

We deserve much better.

12
LETS HEAR IT FOR
THE BOYS

It's not enough for us to note our own greatness. We must also educate the one population who has most misunderstood us – men. We know that lack of education, communication and understanding perpetuate the rape culture. Ignoring, making excuses for, and dismissing acts of aggression against women only hurt society as a whole. Brock Turner stripped a woman who was unconscious on the ground next to a dumpster, raped her, and his father's reaction was to tell a judge that imprisoning his son was a "steep price to pay for 20 minutes out of his 20 plus years of life."

Understandably, he was a father trying to save his own child but what about the victim who testified to now hating her own body, not being able to trust herself or anyone else again, feeling violated, and enduring endless self-hatred as a result of the attack?

One wonders how very differently her father feels about those 20 minutes.

The key here is the two fathers. No question, men have treated women poorly throughout history. But men have also been our friends, our lovers, our educators, our family, our confidants, and our companions. They have been our cheerleaders and our protectors. They have been our inspirations, our heroes, and our co-conspirators.

We owe them the benefit of talking to them more about this important topic.

- Explain to the males in your life what it truly feels like to have a stranger make inappropriate comments to you and why you suddenly feel mute in standing up for yourself.
- Explain how often girls and women hear negative female talk and how it makes you feel.

- Explain that uncomfortable feeling you get when alone and suddenly passing a man on the street, in a hallways, or even how you feel passing men on a public street.
- Tell them the first time someone said something sexually suggestive to you and – most importantly – how young you were.

When men understand the constant barrage under which women (and girls) are assaulted with language, gestures, intonations, media images and song lyrics, they will begin to see how wrong things have been. Perhaps it will change how they also speak and/or think about women.

- Describe to the males in your life how many times you are told to smile.
- Illuminate for the males in your life how often you must consider where to park your car, how to walk, where you choose to go jogging, or even whether to step onto an elevator all based on your personal safety – and it is in the middle of the day or early evening.
- Explain how often you've felt the eyes of your own boss or teacher on your body and how disgusting that makes you feel.

It is not their fault. Because men do not live with this, because they park where they want, jog when they want, and wear what they want, they simply do not understand how different your life is.

Ask that he consider your "In Defense of Women Training Guide for Men." It is direct, simple, smart.

In Defense of Women Training Guide for Men

1. Stop using derogatory female terms to emasculate another male – even in jest.
2. Stop using derogatory words to describe a female that you wouldn't use against a male.
3. Stop assessing females on sexual-conquest appearance. However, should you come face-to-face with MMA fighters Ronda Rousey, Holly Holmes or Joanna Jedrzejczyk, feel free to assess whether you could beat her in a fight (as you might do when assessing other males). It is important to note that you will lose.
4. Make a stand for women. When/if co-workers or friends make sexual comments about a female, huge impact can be made by simply saying, "That's not cool, dude."
5. Make a female friend. Men and women CAN "just" be friends. For those who believe they cannot be friends with the opposite sex, there are much bigger issues of respect and self-esteem at play.
6. Understand that the majority of women do NOT want attention from men they do not know.
7. Do not victim-blame or trivialize sexual assault with such statements of "She was asking for it" or "Look how she was dressed." Sexual assault is a crime and never acceptable.
8. Accept the statistics: One out of every six U.S. women has been the victim of a sexual assault; every eight minutes a child is molested; 13% of rape victims attempt suicide; 70% of rape or sexual assault victims experience significant (to severe) emotional long-term stress. Ninety percent of rapes are committed by a known associate or family member, often by someone the victim trusted thus making it even more devastating to report them.

Men Are Victims, Too

Women are not the only victims of sexual crimes. According to numerous studies, including the U.S. Centers for Disease Control and Prevention, one in every six men is the victim of abusive sexual experiences. Exclusive to rape, the Bureau of Justice Statistics found that one in every 71 men will be raped in his lifetime in the United States. Of this latter report, the number of male victims had always remained roughly the same, somewhere between 5 and 14 percent. In 2013, however, the National Crime Victimization Survey revealed that 38 percent of sexual assaults were against men. Just as the Harvey Weinstein outrage brought forth the #MeToo movement in a great wave, researcher Lara Stemple of the Health and Human Rights Project at UCLA School of Law wondered if the Jerry Sandusky and Penn State sex scandal in 2011 and the subsequent media coverage did not empower more male victims to come forward.[43]

When the language was changed to also include the molestation and/or coercion of boys, including unwanted oral sex, rather than just anal sex, the statistics jumped from one in every 71 men to one in every six – a staggering difference and more evidence in how the "macho" culture adversely affects us all.

And just like their female counterparts, these victims suffer from severe depression, anxiety, fear of public scrutiny and shame, but male victims are far less likely to report the crime and also have higher instances of alcoholism, drug abuse, suicidal thoughts and attempts, and PTSD.[44]

However grim, the hope is this: the more we talk about these horrendous crimes, the more we shift the power.

Let's power on …

13
FIGHT, FLIGHT OR …
FREEZE?

There is yet another reason why victim-blaming is not only intolerable but biologically incorrect: For decades, self-defense taught the "fight or flight" methods, never giving any consideration to the idea of …freezing? To freeze was, in the minds of most, pathetic. It was a total give up and, in the fight world, unforgivable.

New evidence, however, reveals that not only is the freeze instinct real, it is biological. A 2017 study in Stockholm, published in the journal *Acta Obstetricia et Gynecologica Scandinavica*, pokes gaping holes in the archaic arguments that if the victim did not fight back, it was not rape. As recently as late 2016, a judge in Italy ruled in favor of a rapist because his victim did not scream or fight enough to call the attack rape. The victim, who was abused as a child by her father, freezes "with people who are too strong." To add more injury to the victim, she now faces slander charges lodged against her by her assailant.[45]

The Swedish study found that tonic immobility, believed to be an evolutionary defense mechanism in animals (look up fainting goats), may also exist in humans. Tonic immobility causes the body to freeze when the animal or human is unable to fight back. The results of this particular study showed that it was normal for rape victims to experience temporary paralysis, thus rendering them unable to strongly resist or call for help. The study, including almost 300 women who went to an emergency room in Stockholm following assaults, found that 70 percent of the victims experienced tonic immobility during the attack. Of those, 50 percent reported extreme, almost catatonic, paralysis.[46]

How many times have we heard or read about an attack in which the victim reportedly froze, went mute, or described her attack as an out-of-body experience in which she could not move? Yet she would be blamed for not fighting back.

As it happens, the entire "fight or flight" discussion in self-defense, law enforcement, and rape crisis centers around the world, not to mention how lay people weigh in, is hotly debated.

Here are some facts you need to consider:

- Some domestic violence and rape crisis centers teach that that fighting the attacker may cause more harm or even death to the victim. This is misleading. It is true that it could cause more harm because a fight does mean you can be hurt. However, what does it mean if you do not fight?
- One U.S. study examined 1.5 million assault victims over the course of a decade and determined that women who fought back were more likely to get away but the fight did increase incidents of injury by 10%.
- Every scenario, every assault, every victim and every predator is different. Because of this, it is essential that women take self-defense courses to prepare and better enable themselves to read and react to different situations.
- Any self-defense course, book, seminar or instructor who "guarantees" safety is misleading his/her students.
- Not fighting off an attacker leads to greater levels of anxiety, remorse, stress, and guilt. In a study of women who did and did not fight their rapist but were all victims of rape, those who did not fight experienced greater episodes of post-traumatic stress syndrome, recurring nightmares and re-living the attacks, guilt and anxiety.

In the Swedish study, researchers discovered that the victims who experienced tonic immobility or temporary paralysis were at higher risk of PTSD and depression following the rape. And though they could not help their own reaction and immobility to the attack, they then blamed themselves for not fighting back. The long-term emotional damage from this is immeasurable.

The reality is we can talk about what we should do in the event of a predatory attack all day long. Until you are face-to-face with an assailant, you do not know how you will react. It is why the story of Leigh Ann is so wonderful as she turned on her imagined attacker, chasing and barking like a dog to scare him off. It does not matter that she may have been wrong about the man's intentions; she discovered that she would be able to react in her time of need. She has great comfort in this. For women who did not or were physically/emotionally unable to fight back, an unspeakably horrible assault is then compounded by one's own guilt and remorse. This heartbreaking truth is further evidence of how we must educate all people about the realities of rape and the rape culture. That an innocent person could be so tortured by the act of another person and, worse, one who most typically goes free is unacceptable.

It is also another reason to be as proactive as you can in your own welfare. Multiple studies have shown that sexual assault prevention programs combined with self-defense can cut the risk of rape by as much as 50 percent, but there is even more!

A study published in the *Journal of Interpersonal Violence* demonstrated the importance of self-defense training, using data from 3,187 female college students. Women with what the researchers termed pre-assault training were more likely to head off an attack (remember self-awareness and situational awareness), but were also less scared and ready to defend themselves before the assault than those women without any training.[47]

With continued self-defense training and/or sexual assault prevention education comes opportunities to discuss different scenarios, role-play, and better prepare for the what-ifs. These scenarios allow women to become more assertive, confident, and in control – all very empowering tools every woman and man should possess.

Trending slogans and hashtags like #TimesUp! and GirlPower! are wonderful but are just words unless we make it real. This is your time to empower and embolden you!

14
TRUMPING THE RAPE CULTURE
AND
THE ART OF WAR

What is the war? might be the question many would ask in relation to self-defense, but the more appropriate question is *WHY is there a war*? Why do we have a culture that tolerates abuse of its daughters? Why do we have a culture that continuously degrades people? More importantly – and this will indeed happen even with the publication of this work – why would people argue against the end of the rape and blame culture?

In fact, when it comes to the rape and blame cultures, we have nothing but "whys." It is perfect reasoning then to seek not answers (as there are no reasonable ones to be given) but solutions through the ancient work of Sun Tzu's *The Art of War*. Throughout history, the 512 B.C. publication of military strategies has been used as an instructional tool in business, education, military, sports and, now, self-defense. On the surface, the principles of the book are about warfare but, truly, it is about knowing your enemy and understanding your own strategy. This is, of course, the entire principle behind self-defense. Despite the images that come to mind when one speaks about self-defense (throat punches and judo flipping-moves), self-defense IS about knowing your enemy and knowing how to fight/defend/survive.

The following are some of the most basic principles of the author's teachings that have been studied (and followed) for centuries:

Planning
In both *The Art of War* and self-defense, planning is about thinking ahead. This is why you become self and situationally aware; this is why you take courses in sexual assault prevention and defense. Military leader Sun Tzu wrote, "The art of war is of vital importance to the State. It is a matter of life and death, a road either to safety or to ruin." The "state" is you. Sun Tzu continues

71

with, "Hence it is a subject of inquiry which can on no account be neglected." Preparing and caring for your own future and safety should on no account be neglected. This preparation is vital to the road upon you wish to travel. Be proactive in your own life!

Character

You have read about how you project yourself to the outside world. Making eye contact, walking tall, and appearing confident send a definite message. "The greatest victory is that which requires no battle" (Sun Tzu). Even when Leigh Ann charged her imagined assailant, barking like a dog, she was terrified. As brave as the act was, she was terrified. She was proactive in her own perceived on-coming assault and won. In the majority of assaults, however, the attack is perpetuated by a known person. So, ask yourself this: If you were known by friends and family to regularly take self-defense courses and it was also well-known that you would report and prosecute – to the fullest – anyone who inappropriately touched you, wouldn't this increase your odds of safety among those same friends and family?

You must be your greatest cheerleader and personal safety proponent.

Using Advantages

In *The Art of War*, Sun Tzu teaches that through experience comes natural advantages: "One may know how to conquer without being able to do it." By taking sexual harassment and assault courses, by engaging in active self-defense classes, by becoming situationally aware, you are living your own survival strategies. As you have already read, studies show that for those women who attended such classes, their risk of assault dropped over 50 percent. In particular, women who fought back, were able to escape/evade, and/or verbally warned their attacker – roared! – compared to those who did not resist, the risk of rape fell upward to 80 to 98.3 percent.[48]

Strength & Weaknesses

In both martial arts and self-defense, we teach fighters how to fight. Yes, of course, this does mean learning and perfecting certain techniques but, as fighters, it really means learning how to use what works in a fight and how to evade where you are most weak. "Thus the expert in battle moves the enemy, and is not moved by him" (Sun Tzu). Your strength should be recognizing that "vibe" you get from someone and moving away. Your strength can be adopting the rule that you will never be alone with someone you do not know and trust well. Or your strength could be your strength – your ability to fight. Understand and appreciate these strengths, but also realize your weaknesses as these are what your enemy will try to use to harm you. Learn to yell. Learn to roar. Never fear repercussions from an employer or family member when your own personal safety, dignity, and emotional welfare are threatened! "Thus the expert in battle moves the enemy, and is not moved by him" (Sun Tzu).

Deception

In *The Art of War*, Sun Tzu states that all warfare is based on deception. Having the enemy think you are stronger than you are or that you have greater artillery than they or that a battle will take place in a completely different location are all part of military strategy. In self-defense, these rules also apply. You have a friend coming. Your phone is on and everyone knows where to find you. "Victorious warriors win first and then go to war, while defeated warriors go to war first and then seek to win" (Sun Tzu). As you have read so many times in this book, women are assaulted in an act of opportunity. The attacker pounces, thinking little of any repercussions as prior history has proved to him there will be no punishment for his crimes. And this is where your roar comes in: "There's a camera, jackass!" He turns; you run. However it works, do whatever you can do.

Perception

To either the known or unknown aggressor, whether you know this person or it is a blindside attack, be more trouble than you are worth. This is an addendum to the aforementioned **Deception**. "There is no instance of a nation benefitting from prolonged warfare." In other words, according to Sun Tzu, a tired army is a defeated army. If you are in any kind of setting that is public or semi-public, the more you delay, the more trouble the aggressor will have. And the perception that you are in control is daunting.

This is HIS attack, HIS assault. If you are talking about his exit strategy to him, reminding him of the cameras and/or who knows where you are, you can wear him down. In a private dwelling, the threat of a security camera or Amazon's Siri or Google's Smart Speaker listening to the conversation buys valuable time. Just as Sun Tzu hypothesized, "who wishes to fight must first count the cost," remind your assailant that you really are NOT worth his time.

War Games or Prevention

Not to be confused with planning, there is a big difference between learning to walk tall and being self-aware and knowing how to physically defend yourself. First and foremost, learning self and situational awareness is so important. Finding your inner "grrr" is incredible. It is a must for self-protection, but learning to actually move in a way in which you could save your own life is invaluable.

Taking and participating in sexual assault courses is a great first move. But as you actually participate in fight scenarios that allow you to physically react to (not just hear about) different moves and different situations, your mind will slow down and you will be able to better process what is happening. We know that tonic "freezing" immobility is real. There is no guarantee in self-defense, but why not increase your odds? In 2017, my own daughter was assaulted outside her violin studio in Houston, Texas. It was late at night and she had parked around the corner in an unlit area (which she got in big trouble for by her mother!) when she heard a noise and turned to see a man running at her.

Later, still shaking but very much alive and well, she relayed what happened. Her entire life, she has attended my kickbox classes, served as my "attacker" in a few seminars, and has actively participated in countless self-defense classes. So she prepared herself. "It was just like you've always said, Momma. When I turned around and saw him coming, everything just slowed down." She instantly began to process what was happening.

1. *I'm being attacked.*

2. Guards up. Self-defense.
3. *Here he comes.*
4. She used her violin case like a baseball bat, swung hard and won.

Practice can make perfect. As Sun Tzu says, "In the midst of chaos, there is also opportunity." Just as in the case of Leigh Ann discovering her roar, my daughter's constant practice had allowed her to process what was happening to her, break it down, and react in a manner that may have just saved her life.

#MeToo

Full disclosure: Sun Tzu did not know or write about the #MeToo movement. Ah, but he did say, "To win one hundred victories in one hundred battles is not the acme of skill. To subdue the enemy without fighting is the acme of skill."

Within the #MeToo movement, we obviously all wish that each of the women were never assaulted in the first place; but, since they were, we also wish to have seen justice served. Without these deserved outcomes, however, our next strategy – the art of our own war – is to paint a picture of promise for the future:

We educate our youth.
We empower our women.
We change the culture.
We bring criminals to justice.
We give our victims a voice.
We change the laws and how we enable privileged assailants.
We will fight.

15
GAME ON!

At last. The instructional guide to self-defense.

If you ever saw the movie *Karate Kid* (the original 1984 with Ralph Macchio and Noriyuki "Pat" Morita or the 2010 remake with Jaden Smith and Jackie Chan), you are well aware of the quote, "Wax on, wax off. Wax on, wax off."

In the movie, the poor kid, Daniel, just wants to learn karate so he can defend himself against a bully. Mr. Miyagi takes his time introducing any martial arts and instead gives Daniel domestic chores of painting, sanding, and waxing. When the actual lessons in martial arts finally come, Daniel suddenly sees the value in the wax on, wax off movements he has performed so many times.

In real life, anyone can (and should) take self-defense classes. But, more often than not, the participants are just going through the motions. Self-defense is not just about executing a throat punch, flipping someone, or getting out of a choke hold. If those moves become necessary, understand that the assault happens so quickly that most one-time self-defense class graduates typically forget everything they learned and panic. This is why self-defense has to be taken again and again and again. It is also why learning about and understanding – truly understanding – the importance of self and situational awareness; accepting the value of how you present yourself; understanding what predators look for and why; realizing that most sexual assaults are at the hands of a known and once trusted associate, friend, neighbor or relative are so important before you ever throw your first punch.

In the movie (yes, the *Karate Kid* is actually being quoted again because Mr. Miyagi is a bad-ass), Daniel just wants to win the trophy in a local karate tournament to show he can't be messed with, but Mr. Miyagi knows better. He tells the kid, "If karate used to defend honor, defend life, karate mean something. If karate used to defend plastic, metal trophy, karate no mean nothing."

Let's recap. Using the same format I provide in my self-defense seminars, re-introduce yourself to the fundamentals of protecting yourself:

In Defense of Me

- How many of you know someone who has been the victim of a crime? Specifically, the victim of a physical assault?
- Define a "bad guy."
- Define a stranger.
- What does that stranger or "bad guy" look like?
- Define "strong" and "independent" and "confident."
- What is self-esteem?
- What is self-worth?

Definition of Victim:
1. Somebody hurt or killed: somebody who is hurt or killed by somebody or something, especially in a crime, accident, or disaster
2. Somebody or something harmed: somebody who or something that is adversely affected by an action or circumstance
3. Somebody duped: somebody who is tricked or exploited

In self-defense, there are two kinds of victims:
1. Victim of a stranger
2. Victim of a known associate (family member, friend, classmate, neighbor, etc.)

First Line Defense

1. **Definition of Self Defense**: Taking whatever means necessary to stop an attack and put distance between yourself and your attacker!
2. **Objective**:
   - Stop initial attack
   - Strike with maximum amount of force with maximum amount of damage
   - Draw attention to your situation

3. **Strike Zone**: Main strike areas are eyes, throat, groin, and knees

4. **Available weapons**: KNOW YOUR WEAPONS
   - Head
   - Elbows
   - Knees
   - Hands
   - Teeth

5. **Mental Awareness**: Be aware of your surroundings. Always be on the mental defense. (Translation: Put away the iPhone while walking in public.)
6. **Strengths and Weaknesses**: Know your limitations. Know your strengths and advantages. Your number one advantage is surprise and there is no second chance at surprise.
7. Develop skills needed to defend.
8. Develop muscle groups used in this defense.
9. Replace shock with action. Act instead of react.
10. **Develop the attitude to win!**
    - Do not fight to prevent robbery.
    - Fight to save yourself or a loved one.

- Key Words to remember in self-defense:
  - Ruthlessness
  - Determination
  - Physical Fitness
  - Speed
  - Surprise
  - Warrior Mode – Never Quit!
- Do not hesitate to cause pain.
- Attacks can be brutal and savage:
  - Your attack should be just as brutal and savage.
- Never let any concept of fairness cloud your willingness to strike any way you can!
- When you make a defensive move and cause your attacker to hesitate, lose focus or awareness, you MUST use those few seconds to attack.
- Never fight anyone on equal footing. Your attacker is not fighting fair. Nor should you. Use any means necessary to do serious damage and run.
- Anything and everything is a weapon.

- It is a surprise to your attacker if you fight. It is an even bigger surprise to your attacker if you know how to fight.
- If your attacker underestimates your ability to fight, he will be less cautious in his attack, and these initial moments of the attack are crucial!
  - You can have your fingers in his eyes and your knee in his groin before he realizes he is in a fight, not simply an attack.
- A sharp/loud yell along with a well-placed kick or punch will produce results.

- YELLING IS A WEAPON!
  - Screaming in fear is just panic. There is a difference.
  - Animals growl on the attack – it's super scary and super effective!
- You are not a trained police officer. Do not think, "Control. Hold. Restrain." Think. "Immediate damage. Inflict injury. GET OUT!"

- No encounter should last more than 30 seconds.
  - You are fighting to survive. The longer the fight, the greater your chance of losing.
  - You have to want it more than he does!
- Expect to be hurt.
  - Your body is not as frail or delicate as you have been led to believe. Your body was built to endure punishment if it has to.
  - This is not the time to beg or try to negotiate. You have been chosen for a reason. It is – like it or not – officially "game on!" and you are in for the fight of your life. Your only motivation is to find a way to bring attention to yourself and get away.

Remember:
- If an attacker is aroused by hate, anger, rage, lust or any other emotional drive, he has increased power and increased resistance to pain.
- A man is more likely to continue an assault with a broken finger or after being struck in the face than he is after a crushing blow to the groin or the knee, an elbow to the windpipe, or an eye gauge.
- Go for critical targets:

- **Eyes** – eye attacks with the fingers or thumbs cause pain and obstruct vision.
- **Throat** – Regardless of physical strength, everyone reacts to loss of air. Go for windpipe!
- **Groin** – You do not have to use your foot or knee. There is no law against punching.
- **Go for the knee!** The knee joint is easy to hurt and it vital for pursuing prey. Prey is what your attacker considers you to be! But 65 pounds of pressure brought sharply against a straight leg will crack the knee. Attacks to the side of the knee also work against ligaments and tendons.

■ Secondary Targets:
  - Bridge of the nose
  - Side of the neck
  - Shin or instep
  - Spine or kidney
  - Ears
  - Temple

As a 4th degree black belt with more than 30 years in martial arts, a kickbox and self-defense instructor, I do not offer pictures and step-by-step how-to-evade in this book. It is, I believe, dangerous. Nothing annoys me more than to see YouTube videos or magazine pictorials of a large, hulking man cooperatively allowing his female "victim" to use different hand techniques to release his grip on her neck/wrist/shoulder/arm/waist. Watching videos where an otherwise well-intended father demonstrates how his young daughter can "easily" force him to release his vice-like grip on her neck is not accurate, not a true portrayal of how self-defense works. Many of the techniques you see on video would not work the first 50 times you tried them on an aggressive person meaning you harm. Add in confusion and shock, the adrenaline of your attacker, and your chances are greatly minimized.

What I do endorse and what you have now completed is the first step to proactive self-defense training and care of your own being. I hope you read this book again and share with others. I hope you talk about some of the scenarios and then decide to get a friend or two to commit with you to numerous self-defense seminars, self-defense classes, and sexual assault prevention courses. From these classes/courses, women (and men) learn greater self-awareness and greater situational awareness, how to listen to and respect your own gut feelings, and how to walk tall and use your voice. There is a reason why learning self-defense and awareness can reduce your chances of being a victim from 50 to 98.3 percent: You are taking control of your life and your environment. Together, we can trump the rape culture, the blame game, and fight back against those who choose to be predators.

Power on.

Be Kind,
But
Be Fearless!

-Alex

References:

1. Stewart, Emily, "Trump Has Started Suggesting the Access Hollywood Tape is Fake," *VOX*. November 28, 2017

2. Price, S.L., "Why Ben Roethlisberger is the NFL's Most Polarizing Player." *Sports Illustrated*. January 3, 2017.

3. Stern, Marlow, "Kobe Bryant's Disturbing Rape Case: The DNA Evidence, the Accuser's Story, and the Half-Confession." *Daily Beast.* April 11, 2016.

4. Orenstein, Aviva, "Special Issues Raised by Rape Trial." *Fordhams Law Review.* Vol. 76, Issue, 3; article 11, pages 1585-1608. 2007.

5. Orenstein, Aviva, "Special Issues Raised by Rape Trial." *Fordhams Law Review.* Vol. 76, Issue, 3; article 11, pages 1585-1608. 2007

6. http://www.rainn.org/get-information/statistics/reporting-rates

7. Reilly, Steve. "Rape Kits Go Untested," *USA Today.* July 16, 2016. https://www.usatoday.com/story/news/2015/07/16/untested-rape-kits-evidence-across-usa/29902199/

8. https://www.theguardian.com/society/2007/feb/01/penal.genderissues

9. Kaczynski, A., Chris Massie, Nate McDermott. *CNN Radio* Footage of Donald Trump to Howard Stern, October 9, 2016. http://www.cnn.com/2016/10/08/politics/trump-on-howard-stern/index.html

10. Quinn, Liam. "Trump Caught Bragging About How He Was Able to Get Away with 'Inspecting' Contestants," *Daily Mail.* October 9, 2016.

11. https://www.ncbi.nlm.nih.gov/pubmed/1635092

12. Bureau of Justice Statistics: https://www.bjs.gov/index.cfm?ty=tp&tid=92

13. https://www.huffingtonpost.com/entry/a-running-list-of-the-women-whove-accused-donald-trump-of-sexual-misconduct_us_57ffae1fe4b0162c043a7212

14. Blakely, Rhys, "It Was the Dirtiest I Ever Felt," *The Times.* December 12, 2017. https://www.thetimes.co.uk/article/it-was-the-dirtiest-i-ever-felt-three-women-accuse-trump-of-sex-abuse-60rwwg780

15. https://www.cbsnews.com/news/thousands-push-for-judge-in-stanford-sex-assault-case-to-be-removed-brock-turner

16. Grimes, David Robert. "Guns Don't Offer Protection" *The Guardian.* March 25, 2013. https://www.theguardian.com/science/blog/2013/mar/25/guns-protection-national-rifle-association

17. John Hopkins Bloomberg School of Public Health
https://www.jhsph.edu/research/centers-and-institutes/johns-hopkins-center-for-gun-policy-and-research/publications/IPV_Guns.pdf

18. Hodnett, Gentry, "Guns & Rape Prevention: A Dangerous Myth". March, 17, 2016. http://ocrcc.org/guns-rape-prevention-a-dangerous-myth/

19. https://www.npr.org/2016/10/14/497953012/jumped-out-of-my-skin-trump-accuser-jessica-leeds-on-why-she-came-forward

20. http://modelmugging.org/self-defense-for-women/

21. https://warriorpublications.wordpress.com/2015/06/16/women-trained-to-resist-sexual-assault-far-less-likely-to-be-raped-study/

22. Crisell, Hattie, "What Female Gamers Want You to Know About Being Abused Online," *BuzzFeed* . February 17, 2016.

23. http://www.notinthekitchenanymore.com/

24. Cauterucci, Christina, "Do Women Like Being Sexually Harassed? Men in New Survey Say Yes." *Slate Magazine*. June 19, 2017

25. Stuart, Tessa, "A Timeline of Donald Trump's Creepiness While He Owned Miss Universe." *Rolling Stone Magazine*. October 12, 2016

26. Love, David A., "The Bully-in-Chief," *The Philadelphia Citizen*. February 6, 2017.

27. https://www.splcenter.org/20161128/trump-effect-impact-2016-presidential-election-our-nations-schools

28. https://assets2.hrc.org/files/assets/resources/HRC_PostElectionSurveyofYouth.pdf

29. http://www.utdallas.edu/news/2015/8/25-31660_UT-Dallas-Criminologist-Tackles-Perception-of-NFL-_story-wide.html

30. https://www.rainn.org/statistics/criminal-justice-system

31. http://www.northeastern.edu/rugglesmedia/2016/10/28/sports-and-cultures-of-violence-a-look-back-at-major-incidents

32. Paresky, Pamela B., Phd, "What's Wrong with Locker Room Talk? Boys will be Boys," *Psychology Today*. October 10, 2016.

33. https://www.webroot.com/us/en/home/resources/tips/digital-family-life/internet-pornography-by-the-numbers

34. Casserly, Meghan. "Science Proves that Women are Mean (Again). Thanks, Science!" *Forbes*. November 29, 2011.

35. Schwartz, Mel, L.C.S.W. "Self Esteem or Other Esteem," *Psychology Today*. July 29, 2013.

36. Locker, Melissa. "Boys May Actually Be Meaner than Girls, Study Says," *Time Magazine*. December 3, 2014.

37. Petter, Olivia. "Women are Kinder and More Generous Than Men, Study Finds," *Independent*. October 10, 2017.

38. Oxford Reference, "Queen Bee Philosophy." *Oxford University Press.* http://www.oxfordreference.com/view/10.1093/oi/authority.2011080310 0358381

39. Forrest, S., V. Eatough, M. Shevlin, "Measuring Adult Indirect Aggression: The Development and Psychometric Assessment of the Indirect Aggression Scales." *Aggressive Behavior.* Vol. 31, pages 84-97, 2005.

40. http://she-conomy.com/facts-on-women

41. United Nations Women: Women's Leadership and Political Participation. http://www.unwomen.org/~/media/headquarters/attachments/sections/lib rary/publications/2013/12/un%20womenlgthembriefuswebrev2%20pdf.a shx

42. Inter-Parliamentary Union (2008): Equality in Politics: A Survey of Men and Women in Parliaments. http://archive.ipu.org/pdf/publications/equality08-e.pdf

43. Rosin, Hanna. "When Men Are Raped: A New Study Reveals that Men Are Often the Victims of Sexual Assault," *Slate.* April 29, 2014.

44. The One in Six Statistics. http://1in6.org/get-information/the-1-in-6-statistic/

45. Phillips, Kristine. "A Sexual Assault Case was Tossed Because the Woman Didn't Scream During Alleged Attack," *Washington Post.* March 26, 2017.

46. Pearson, Catherine. "Why So Many Rape Victims Don't Simply 'Fight Back'," *HuffPost.* August 4, 2017.

47. Brecklin, L, Ullman, S.E., "Self-Defense or Assertiveness Training and Women's Responses to Sexual Attacks." *Journal of Interpersonal Violence.* 2005 June; Vol. 20 (6): pages 738-62.

48. https://www.nij.gov/topics/crime/rape-sexual-violence/campus/Pages/decrease-risk.aspx

About the Author

Not one to shy from a challenge, Alexandra Allred was introduced to the sport of bobsledding by way of her couch. Holding her then six month old daughter, Allred was watching ESPN when she discovered that women were not in the Olympic Games as the sport was deemed too dangerous for women. As a former fighter and a black belt (now a 4th degree), she began her own letter writing campaign and new fight: Get women into the Olympic Games.

Allred was invited to the first-ever U.S. national training camp in 1994 at the Olympic Training Center in Lake Placid, New York. Seven months later, and also 4 ½ months pregnant with her second child, Allred won U.S. Nationals, becoming the country's first female champion. She competed on the World Cup and continued to champion for women in bobsled until the announcement: Women would debut in the 2002 Olympic Games.

Allred played as a women's professional football player for the Austin Rage (#RageOn), and was asked to test drive/write about the Volvo Gravity Car as an adventure writer. She worked with Erin Brokovich, Earthjustice and Downwinders at Risk to combat irresponsible emissions of toxic materials by big industry, and was nominated for the White House Champion of Change for Public Health and Prevention. Allred testified before the EPA and US Senators but never left her primary goals of empowering women. Throughout, Allred continued to offer self-defense classes and adopted the philosophy, "be kind but be fearless." "One does not have to change the essence of who they are to become a badass."

Allred returned to school to earn her Masters in Kinesiology in 2016 to teach those living with special needs and to work with seniors citizens for greater functional movement. She teaches these amazing group self-defense and is also a survivor.

Trumping Your Attacker

CPSIA information can be obtained
at www.ICGtesting.com
Printed in the USA
LVHW04s0002290618
582260LV00001B/67/P

9 781941 398180